cocktail deluxe

cocktail deluxe

MARIA COSTANTINO

SB

Published by SILVERDALE BOOKS
An imprint of Bookmart Ltd
Registered number 2372865
Trading as Bookmart Ltd
Desford Road
Enderby
Leicester LE19 4AD

D&S Books Ltd
Kerswell,
Parkham Ash, Bideford
Devon, England
EX39 5PR

e-mail us at:-
enquiries@dsbooks.fsnet.co.uk

This edition printed 2003

ISBN 1-856057-78-X

DS0073 Cocktail Deluxe

Creative Director: Sarah King
Project editor: Anna Southgate
Photographer: Colin Bowling
Designer: Axis Design Editions

Fonts used in thos book: Pike,
Didot and Helvetica.

Printed in China

1 3 5 7 9 10 8 6 4 2

Contents

Introduction

If you like cocktails and mixed drinks, then you'll love the recipes included in this book. These delicious drinks are in fact very easy to make, but some of the ingredients may be a little unfamiliar. Don't worry though: by the time you have read through the next couple of pages you'll be able to identify all the interesting-looking bottles, know where they come from, how their contents are made and, most important, what they taste like!

These – and all alcoholic drinks – are meant to accompany good times with good friends, not be the good time (or good friend) in themselves. Before you begin reading any further, take a moment to consider the responsible use and serving of alcoholic drinks.

Responsible drinking is the key to enjoyment, health and safety – both yours and that of others, especially if you are a driver. Remember, the only person who can safely handle a pint while driving is a milkman!

Do not condone or encourage underage drinking: there are numerous non-alcoholic 'fruity' syrups that can be used to create delicious 'mocktails'. You will find that these are very popular with many people because they are so tasty, so be prepared, when you entertain, to provide them for all your guests!

Do not 'push' an alcoholic drink onto a guest: if they say no, they mean no. Offer delicious juices and sparkling minerals instead, and never, ever, 'spike' anyone's drink: they may be the designated driver that night, be allergic to alcohol, be on medication, have religious beliefs which preclude alcohol or may be 'in recovery'. After all, you invited all your guests because they were friends and you like them, not because they drink!

The Basics:

The key to making delicious cocktails and mixed drinks involves a couple of simple rules:

Keep your ingredients cool: chill juices and mixers, champagnes and vermouths. Aquavits and vodkas are best if they are very cold.

Wash mixing equipment between making different cocktails to avoid mixing flavours. Rinse spoons and stirrers too!

Have all the equipment – can opener, bottle opener, shaker, jigger, mixing glass, bar spoon, straws, stirrers – ready to hand.

Prepare glasses, fruit juices, fruit garnishes and ingredients like sugar syrup, lemon or lime juices and coconut cream in advance of your guests arriving.

Make sure you have plenty of ice: an ice bucket is ideal and insulation is vital. A well-insulated, capacity ice bucket is better than a 'novelty' design which results in a bucket of melted ice! Tongs are more efficient than a spoon for taking ice from the bucket: you won't get any extra – and unwanted – water.

Measures

In this book you will see that the recipes call for 1 measure, or ½ measure of a spirit or liqueur. The word measure is used because of the slight variations between metric, British Imperial and US measurements, and because each side of the Atlantic has a variation on the fluid ounce. Since most of the classic cocktails were invented in America, the 'jigger' used in bars in the USA is often a common measurement. It really doesn't matter what 'jigger' you use – you could use a shot glass, or even an egg cup as your 'measure'. As long as you use the same measure throughout, the ratios of one spirit to another in your drink will be correct. It's a good idea, though, to measure – using water – the total quantities of a drink and pour them into the glass to make sure all the contents fit!

Equipment

There are three basic pieces of equipment that you'll need to make cocktails: a shaker, a mixing glass and a blender.

Drinks made with ingredients such as eggs, cream, sugar syrup and fruit are shaken and strained to remove any bits of ice or fruit that may spoil the look of a drink. There are two types of shaker: the standard shaker has a built-in strainer, which is very convenient and easy to use but be careful that the seal doesn't leak and that the parts are assembled tightly before you shake! A Boston shaker consists of two flat-bottomed cones: one fits into the other and the liquid needs to be strained through a Hawthorn strainer that is designed to fit over one of the cones.

A mixing glass is used for drinks that require stirring before they are poured – or strained – into the drinking glass. 'Professional' mixing glasses are designed to be used with the Hawthorn strainer, but you can use the bottom section of your standard shaker, then fit the strainer part and strain the drink through that. Alternatively, you could use a glass jug and a fine mesh sieve to pour the drink through. Either method is fine.

A blender is ideal for making drinks with crushed ice, fresh fruits, ice cream and milk, and which require a more thorough blending. When you blend a cocktail, the aim is to produce a drink with a milkshake-like consistency. Too much blending will dilute the drink because crushed ice liquifies very quickly. You can also use a blender if you want to make up a large batch of drinks: to serve a batch of the same drink, set up all the glasses in row in advance. Pour the drink until each glass is half full, then backtrack until the 'shaker' or 'blender jug' is empty. That way every one gets the same amount, thoroughly mixed.

The standard shaker comprises three parts: a lid, which can also double as a measure, a sieve and the base vessel.

In addition to these you will need:

Can and bottle opener/corkscrew
Long-handled bar spoon
A small, sharp paring knife for cutting fruit garnishes
A measuring spoon – for measuring 'dry' sugar
A jigger or your chosen measure
An ice bucket and tongs
Assorted straws, swizzle sticks, muddlers and cocktail sticks to spear garnishes
Glasses

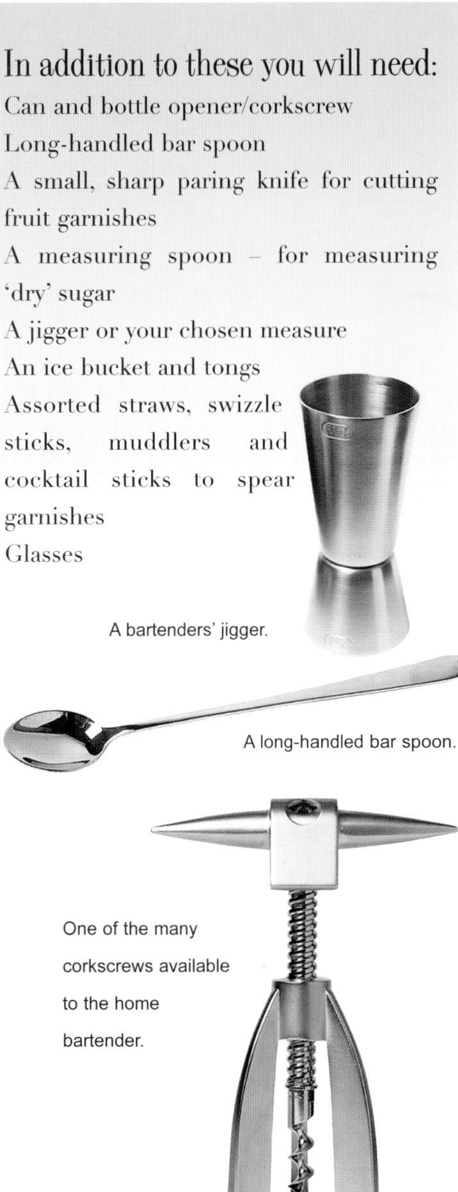

A bartenders' jigger.

A long-handled bar spoon.

One of the many corkscrews available to the home bartender.

Ice

You can't make cocktails without ice, and because it is a vital ingredient it is important that you don't 'skimp' on it. You will need ice cubes, broken ice and crushed ice, depending on the cocktail you select. The object is to almost freeze the drink while breaking down and combining the ingredients.

Broken ice is easy to make: Put some whole ice cubes in a clean polythene bag and hit them with a rolling pin! The aim is to break and ice cube into three pieces. If you want crushed ice, you can keep on hitting, or you can put broken ice into your blender – but only if the instruction booklet says your blender can cope. Most of the blenders on the market today can do this, and some make a feature of their ice-crushing capabilities. Ice will melt quickly so make broken and crushed iced immediately before use and help it along by chilling the drinking glasses.

A good, large and well-insulated ice bucket is essential.

A Word on Methods

Chilling and Frosting Glasses

The simple rule of cocktails is 'chill before you fill'! There are three ways to make a glass cold:

1) Put the glasses in the fridge or freezer for a couple of hours before using them – but don't do this with fine crystal glasses because they can shatter.

2) Fill the glasses with crushed ice before using them. Discard the ice and shake out any water before pouring in the drink.

3) Fill the glasses with cracked ice and 'stir' it round a little before discarding it and pouring in the drink.

There are two types of 'frosted' glasses. For frosted drinks, the glasses should be stored in the fridge or better, buried in shaved ice, to give them a white, frosted and ice-cold appearance. A 'sugar', 'salt' or 'coconut' frosted glass is prepared by moistening the rim with a little lemon or lime juice and then dipping the rim into the condiment.

When a recipes tells you to 'add the ingredients' to a shaker, glass or blender, get into the habit of putting the 'cheapest' ingredients in first! Put lemon or lime juice, sugar syrup and fruit juices in first, then the more valuable spirits and liqueurs. This means that if you make a mistake, chances are it will be with the less expensive ingredients!

Don't, whatever you do, shake a drink with carbonated mixers – ginger ale, tonic or soda water, or even champagne! This type of ingredient is left right until the last and is used to 'finish' a drink.

Where a method says 'shake and strain', half fill the shaker with clean ice cubes, add the ingredients and shake briskly – until the outside of your shaker is very cold! Pour immediately through the strainer, leaving the ice behind. The volume of liquid will have increased because some of the ice will have melted and blended with the other ingredients. Remember this, so you don't produce more drink than your glass will hold.

Don't shake and strain with crushed ice: the crushed ice will just get stuck in the strainer holes and clog them up. Drinks shaken with crushed ice are poured 'unstrained' into the glass.

Where a method says 'shake and pour unstrained', add a glassful of ice to the shaker, pour in the ingredients and shake. Pour the drink into the same-size glass that you used to measure the ice.

Where a recipe instructs you to 'stir and strain', half fill the mixing glass, or the bottom half of your shaker with ice cubes, add the ingredients and stir with the long-handled bar spoon for 10 to 15 seconds. Use a Hawthorn strainer, the strainer part of your shaker or even a mesh sieve and pour the drink through it into the glass.

Where you are instructed to 'stir and pour unstrained', prepare as above, but only use a glassful of ice and don't strain. Add all the contents to a same -size glass as the one you used to measure the ice.

A streamlined cocktail shaker.

To 'build' a drink means that you are creating the drink directly in the glass in which it will be served. Some drinks are built 'over ice' – the ice cubes are added to the glass first and the liquors added – others are made as a 'pousse-café'. A pousse-café makes use of the difference in the 'weights' of liqueurs and spirits so that one sits on top of the other forming separate, often coloured, layers. This can be a little fiddly to do at first, but the results can be spectacular. The trick is to pour the liquors very slowly over the back (the rounded side) of a small spoon, so that it very gently sits on top of the layer before it.

Pouring

Pour drinks as soon as you make them or they will 'wilt' (become too diluted with melted ice) and, in some instances, separate into their component parts.

Adding a Twist

When a recipe calls for a twist of lemon, lime or orange peel, rub a narrow strip of peel around the rim of the glass to deposit the oil on it. Then twist the peel so that the oil – usually one very small drop – falls into the drink. In some recipes, you then drop the peel into the glass, while in others you discard the peel.

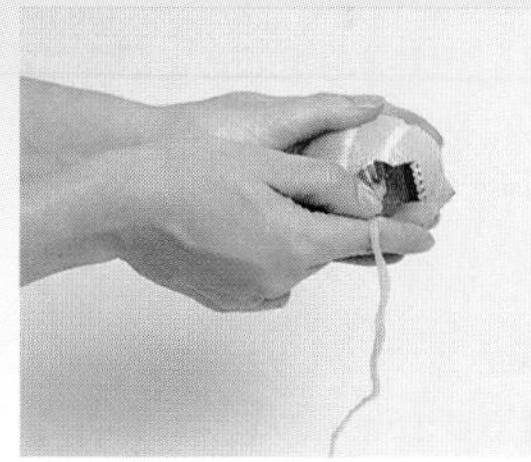

Glasses

All your glasses must be spotlessly clean! Test each type of glass to see how much it holds – this will allow you to adjust your measure and quantities so the final drink will fit the glass perfectly. Using the 'correct' glass ensures not only visual impact, but guarantees the right glass is used to serve the drink for which it was designed: a brandy snifter is shaped so that the liquor is gently warmed by the hands; a champagne flute is designed to keep the bubbles in the glass; a straight-sided pousse-café glass helps maintain the separate layers. For each recipe, you will find the type of glass recommended for the particular drink, and where possible, an alternative suggestion. The type of glass is important for the drink, the style – and size – of each type is a matter of personal taste! The most commonly recommend glass types are:

Cocktail: Elegant and stemmed to protect the chilled contents from the heat of hands. It usually holds bout 5 fl oz (125 ml). A double cocktail glass is slightly larger and holds around 8 fl oz (225 ml).

Old-fashioned: Sometimes called a tumbler or whisky glass, this is a short, chunky 'tumbler', holding around 8 fl oz (225 ml).

Highball: A tall glass, normally containing around 8 fl oz (225 ml).

Collins: Narrow, very tall, often with straight sides, and designed for long drinks. Typically contains about 10 fl oz (250 ml).

Pilsner: A beer glass, but not the 'beer mug' seen in British pubs. This is the glass that German and other continental lagers are traditionally served in. Typically, about 10 fl oz (250 ml).

Champagne Saucer: This is the 'open' cup-shaped glass seen in the movies. It is said the shape was inspired by the French queen, Marie Antoinette's breasts! This holds about 5 fl oz (125 ml).

Champagne Flute: This is the tall, thin and stemmed glass – sometimes called a tulip – that holds around 5 fl oz (125 ml).

Shot Glass: These are the little, individual glasses used to serve 'shooters' and shots of ice-cold vodka and aquavit.

Parfait Glass: This is a small and stemmed glass for liqueurs and cordials. They normally hold between 1 and 2 fl oz (25 and 50 ml).

Cordial Glass: This is sometimes called a 'pony' and it looks like a very small white wine glass. It holds about 2 fl oz (50 ml) and is used for serving liqueurs.

Goblet: Basically this is a large-bowled glass on a shortish stem, that holds around 12 fl oz (325 ml). You can, however, use a large wine glass, or indeed any attractive 'wide-mouthed' glass, like a piña colada or hurricane glass (see below) since many of the drinks served in these glasses are rich and creamy.

Piña Colada or Poco: This glass is the traditional vessel for the famous coladas. It has a very distinctive shape and holds a hefty 14 fl oz (375 ml).

Hurricane: This glass is similar to the piña colada glass, but is often a little less rounded – more elongated. In fact, it looks similar to the hurricane lamp from which it gets its name. You can interchange a goblet, a piña colada, a hurricane or even a large wine glass – your drinks will look just as spectacular and taste equally magnificent.

Attractive and sparkling glassware adds visual impact to a drink.

The Well-stocked Bar

The basis for many cocktails, no matter how exotic, remains a spirit. These are mixed with each other, with liqueurs, with fruit juices, with eggs, with cream or coconut cream to produce the thousands of exciting combinations available today. Look through the recipes and find the 'flavours' that interest you: then look at the ingredients to see what you need. Don't forget that you can also get many of these spirits and liqueurs in 'miniatures': tiny, but perfectly formed, single measures that are ideal if you want to try out a cocktail without splashing out on a big bottle!

Spirits

Bitters: The term bitters refers to a number of spirits flavoured with bitter herbs and roots. These range from products like Campari – which can be drunk in whole measures like any other spirit or mixed with other ingredients like Fernet-Branca and Amer Picon – to bitters that are added in drops to 'season' a drink. The most famous of these 'dropping' bitters are undoubtedly angostura bitters, made from a secret Trinidadian recipe; Peychaud bitters made in New Orleans; and Abbot's Aged bitters made in Baltimore, Maryland since 1865. There are also orange bitters made by numerous companies.

Brandy and Cognac: Both are spirits made from distilled grape wine. Brandy can be made in any country where vines are grown –

Pisco is a clear brandy from Peru and Chile – but Cognac can only come from the Cognac region in France, where the brandy is made from white wines and distilled in traditional pot stills before maturing in oak casks. Cognacs are labelled: VSO (Very Superior Old) VSOP (Very Superior Old Pale) VVSOP (Very, Very Superior Old Pale) and XO (Extremely Old).

Armagnac: This is a grape brandy produced in this region in southwest France and which uses only three specified white wines: Haut Armagnac (white), Tenareze and Bas Armagnac (black). If the spirit is described simply as 'Armagnac' it is a blend of these three types.

Calvados: This is an apple brandy made in Normandy, France; Applejack is an American apple brandy – sometimes known as Jersey Lightning – after the state where it is produced. It is sold straight or blended with neutral spirits.

Eau de Vie: This is a spirit produced from fruit other than grapes and apples: it is a colourless (because it has not been aged in wooden casks) fruit brandy, most often made from soft berries such as raspberries, strawberries, pears and cherries. Eau de vie is not sweetened and should not be confused with its syrupy liqueur cousin, (often made using one of the same fruits) although this tends to be coloured anyway!

Whisky: (Scotch and Canadian) and whiskey (Irish, American and Japanese).

Bourbon: This is a generic term for a bourbon-style American whiskey, distilled in a continuous still method from fermented cereal mash containing a minimum of 51% corn and aged for 6 to 8 years in oak casks.

Canadian Whisky: This is made from cereal grains such as barley, corn, rye and wheat in varying proportions depending on the manufacturer, in a continuous still method and aged for six years.

Irish Whiskey: Similar to Scotch, the difference here is that the barley is dried in a kiln rather than over a peat fire.

Rye Whiskey: Produced in both Canada and the USA, rye is distilled from a mixture of cereals but no less than 51% rye.

Scotch: Blended Scotch is a mixture of grain spirit – usually maize – and one or more malt whiskies. The malt whisky is made from barley which has germinated, been dried over smoky peat fires, mashed, fermented, distilled and aged in wooden casks for 10 to 12 years or more.

Vodka: This is an almost neutral spirit distilled from a fermented mash of grain, which is filtered through charcoal. There are colourless and odourless varieties as well as subtly flavoured and aromamtised versions such as bison grass vodka, cherry vodka, lemon vodka, and pepper vodka.

Gin: London dry gin is made form a distillate of unmalted grain. The spirit is infused with juniper and other 'botanicals' before and during distillation to produce a gin with a subtle flavour and aroma. London dry gin is therefore a 'style' of gin as there are many famous brands to choose from such as Gordon's, Bombay Sapphire and Beefeater. Plymouth Gin is made only in Plymouth, England and is the traditional gin used for a 'pink gin'. This is produced by Coates at the Blackfriar's distillery in the city. Sloe gin – and its French equivalent prunelle – is not a spirit but a liqueur made of sweetened gin in which the fruit (sloes) of the blackthorn bush have been steeped and then strained out after they have stained the spirit a deep red. (Prunelle is green however!). Dutch genever sometimes called 'Hollanders gin' is very different to English gin because it uses a more pungent grain mash that is quite heavily malted. There are two grades: '*oude*' (old) and '*jonge*' (young), the latter looking a little less beer-coloured and more like English gin.

Rum: This is the distilled spirit of fermented sugar cane sap. The cane is crushed to remove the sap, the water allowed to evaporate off, and the resulting syrup is spun in a centrifuge to separate out the molasses which are extracted, reduced by boiling, then fermented and distilled. The exceptions to this method are rums from Haiti and Martinique, which are made from reduced but otherwise unprocessed sugar cane sap. Dark rum is matured for about five years in barrels previously used for bourbon. The rum is then blended and sometimes caramel is added to darken the colour. White rum is a clear, colourless, light-bodied rum: the molasses are fermented then distilled in a column still to produce the spirit, which is aged for just one year before bottling. Golden rum is produced in the same way as white rum, but is aged for around three years in charred barrels which give the rum its golden hue and mellow flavour.

Tequila and Mescal: Tequila is a spirit distilled in the region of the same name in Mexico from the cactus-like plant *agave tequilana*. The heart of the cactus is harvested, steam-cooked and crushed to remove the juice, which is then fermented and double distilled. Silver tequila is matured briefly in stainless-steel or wax-lined vats so it remains colourless – and a little coarse. Gold tequila is matured in oak vats for three or more years where it develops a more mellow flavour and a golden colour. Mescal is the juice or pulque of the agave cactus which is distilled only once (not twice as in tequila). It is often sold bottled with an accompanying pickled, white, agave worm – which is supposed to be eaten! If you can stomach mescal, you can probably stomach the worm as well!

Kirsch: This is the original 'cherry spirit' – a true brandy or eau de vie – made from cherries, and is normally regarded as a 'separate' product to other fruit brandies/eau de vie. It is a particular speciality of Bavaria in western Germany: '*Kirsch*' means 'cherry'. But remember, Kirsch is colourless, and is not related to the bright red and sweet, syrupy 'cherry brandy' liqueurs (see below).

Aquavit or Akavit: This is a grain- and/or potato-based spirit that has been aromatised with fragrant spices like caraway seeds, fennel, cumin, dill and bitter oranges. The Scandinavian countries and Germany produce the true 'aquavits' which are often called 'schnapps', a name derived from the old Nordic word '*snappen*', meaning to snatch or seize, and denotes the traditional way of drinking – down in one gulp! In Denmark Aalborg produces a premium high-stregnth (42% ABV) aquavit, while Archers produces a well-known range of less strong (around 23% ABV) fruit-flavoured schnapps.

Liqueurs

Advocaat: A liqueur that originated in the Netherlands made of a base spirit and sweetened egg yolks.

Amaretto: An almond-flavoured liqueur. The most famous brand is Disaronno amaretto, but other amarettos are also available.

Anisette: A french, sweetened and aniseed-flavoured liqueur, the most famous brand of which is Marie Brizard.

Baileys Irish Cream: A sweet, cream liqueur (as distinct from a creme liqueur, see below) made with whiskey and cream and flavoured with coffee. Baileys is the most well-known proprietary brand.

Benedictine: A bright, golden, aged liqueur using a secret recipe of 75 herbs.

Chartreuse: An ancient French liqueur made by monks. There are two colours: green Chartreuse, which is intensely powerful and aromatic, and yellow Chartreuse, which is sweeter and slightly minty in flavour.

Coconut Rum: This is a sweet, white rum-based liqueur flavoured with coconut. The most well-known proprietary brand is Malibu, but coconut rum is made throughout the Caribbean rum-producing countries. Rum tree is also based on white rum but is a sweet, citrus-flavoured liqueur.

Cointreau: Properly speaking, this very popular branded liqueur is a form of Curaçao (see below): a brandy-based spirit, flavoured with the peel of bitter oranges. It can be served straight up, on the rocks and in mixed drinks where it is used in place of triple sec (see below).

Creme Liqueurs: These are sweetened liqueurs – as distinct from dry spirits like whisky or cognac – and consist of one dominant flavour, often, but not always, fruit: there are also nut-flavoured liqueurs. The most commonly used creme liqueurs are:

Creme de Banane: a sweet clear, yellow banana liqueur. A banana liqueur made from green bananas is pisang ambon, a product of Indonesia.

Creme de Cacao: Chocolate flavoured and available in two varieties: Dark (a distillate of cocoa beans and, sometimes, vanilla, macerated in alcohol, diluted and sweetened, and light, which has a more subtle flavour and is colourless because the cocoa remains are absent.

Creme de Cassis: A blackcurrant-flavoured liqueur.

Creme de Menthe: White and green liqueurs distilled from a concentrate of mint leaves. The white version is more subtle than the green which gets its colour from and added colorant.

Creme de Fraise: A strawberry-flavoured liqueur.

Creme de Framboise: A raspberry-flavoured liqueur.

Curaçao: Originally, a white-rum-based liqueur flavoured with the peel of bitter green oranges found on the island of Curaçao. Today it is made by a number of companies with brandy as the base spirit. A variant name was triple sec (the most famous being Cointreau) but, confusingly, Curaçao is not sec (dry) but always sweet. Curaçao comes in a range of colours as well as the clear version: orange, red, yellow, green and blue. Whatever the colour they all taste of orange and they do add a wonderful colour to mixed drinks and cocktails.

Drambuie: A Scotch-whisky-based liqueur flavoured with heather, honey and herbs.

Galliano: This is a golden yellow liqueur from Italy made to a secret recipe of some 80 herbs, roots and berries, with the principal flavourings being liquorice, anise and vanilla.

Glayva: Like Drambuie (see above) Glavya is a Scotch-whisky-based liqueur, flavoured with honey and herbs.

Grand Marnier: The is France's Cognac-based Curaçao (see above), made with the juice of Caribbean oranges and top-quality Cognac, and cask aged.

Kahlua: A dark-brown coffee-flavoured liqueur from Mexico.

Kümmel: A pure grain distillate – effectively a type of vodka – in which caraway seeds are infused to produce a spearmint-flavoured liqueur made in Latvia, Poland, Germany, Denmark, the Netherlands and in the USA. Goldwasser, made in Gdansk, Poland, has flakes of real gold in it.

Liqueur Brandies: There are essentially three fruit brandies: cherry, apricot and peach (although this last is not often seen). These are not 'true' brandies, but sweetened and coloured liqueurs based on simple grape brandy that has been flavoured with the relevant fruit – as opposed to being distillates of the fruit itself.

Mandarine Napoleon: This is also a type of Curaçao (see above), but this time made with skins of tangerines steeped in Cognac and other French brandies before being coloured to a vivid yellow-orange with carotene and matured for several months. Mandarine Napoleon, the leading brand, is in fact made in Belgium.

Maraschino: This is a clear, colourless liqueur derived from an infusion of pressed cherries and cherrystone distillate and aged for several years. Originally, marasca cherries grown in Dalmatia were used but when this area became part of the Venetian 'empire' plantings of the marasca cherry trees were established in the Veneto area of Italy. A number of Italian companies produce maraschino including Luxardo (in straw covered flasks), Drioli and Stock.

Melon Liqueur: A bright green, sweet and syrupy liqueur, the most famous of which is the Japanese brand Midori. The flavouring agent is melon, but the bright green is achieved through the use of vegetable dyes. First devised in the 1980s, Midori is one of the most recent 'inventions' in liqueurs to hit the cocktail scene.

Pastis: A traditional drink of the Mediterranean countries from Spain to Greece and beyond, and where it is known by a variety of names, pastis is an old French word meaning 'muddled', 'hazy' or 'unclear'. Pernod and Ricard are the most well-known brands, and there is also anise (which is dry); Spain has ojen (pronounced 'oh-hen'), and anis, which can be both sweet and dry; Greece has ouzo. The principal flavouring agent in these is either liquorice or aniseed, along with other herbal ingredients, which are steeped in a neutral alcohol base. Arak, (or raki, in Turkey, Greece and the Balkan countries) which can be found in Java, Borneo, and Sumatra is not a liqueur, but a spirit that can be up to 50% alcohol by volume distilled from a variety of different 'sources' (depending on the raki's country of origin) including sugar cane, rice, figs and plums. Sambuca is an Italian aniseed-flavoured liqueur made from anise, herbs and roots.

Ratafia: This was the 'forerunner' of the liqueur: nuts and fruits steeped in a sweetened spirit base. Today the term ratafia has come to mean a brandy mixed with fresh fruit juices, and made in France. Pineau des Charentes – which comes in both white and rosé varieties – is made in the Cognac region; in Armagnac, they make their own version called Floc de Gascogne, while in the Calvados region of Normandy, fresh apple juice is fortified with the local apple brandy and called Pommeau.

Southern Comfort: America's foremost liqueur using American whiskey and peaches in a recipe that is a closely guarded secret. The practice of blending peach juice and whiskey was common in the bars of the southern states of America in the 19th century and this no doubt played its part in the creation of one of the most popular liqueurs. Unusually for a liqueur, Southern Comfort has a high bottled strength – 40% ABV.

Tia Maria: A dark, sweet, coffee-flavoured liqueur from Jamaica based on dark Jamaican rum that's at least five years old, Blue Mountain coffee and local spices. As well as mixing well in many cocktails, Tia Maria is also popular 'straight up' – or drizzled over chocolate desserts!

Van der Hum: This is the South African equivalent of Curaçao (see above) which used Cape brandy and tangerine-like oranges, known locally as *naartjies*.

The liqueurs listed above are just a few of the most well known, but why not look out for some of the more 'obscure' types such as: La Vielle Cure ('The Old Rectory'); Verveine du Velay (a little like Chartreuse in that it comes in green and yellow varieties); Trappistine, made by Trappist monks in the convent of the Abbaye de Grace de Dieu in Doubs, eastern France, near the border with Switzerland; Fiori d'Alpi made in northern Italy with a little gnarled tree in each bottle!; Curant y Tres from eastern Spain; and Cynar from Italy and made with artichokes!

Wines and Fortified Wines

Fortified wines are wines that have been strengthened by the addition of a spirit - usually a grape spirit. The world's classic fortified wines such as Madeira, Marsala, muscat and muscatel each have their own method of production and the majority are made from white grapes – the most notable exception however is port. Sherry contains only wine and grape spirit, but vermouth – and related products – contain a number of aromatising ingredients.

Vermouth: The cocktail bar would be nothing without vermouth. There are French vermouths and Italian vermouths, and there are dry and sweet vermouths, as well as white or 'bianco', rosé and rosso vermouths. The most well-known brands of dry, white vermouths are from Martini from Italy, and Noilly Prat and Lillet from France. Cinzano produce the well-known bianco vermouth which is sweet. Red vermouths are produced by Cinzano, Martini and by Carpano, who make Punt e Mes, a deep-red bitter vermouth from Turin. Dubonnet from France – which can be either red or white – is also a version of vermouth.

Some recipes have been created using a particular brand of spirit, fortified wine, or liqueur. You will find these specified in some recipes, but don't feel obliged to use them! However, the ingenious bartenders who created the drinks in the first place selected these named products specifically for their individual qualities of flavour and aroma.

In the recipes in this book, only one wine is included: champagne. True champagne must be made by the champagne method – the sparkle is made by secondary fermentation in the bottle, not in a vat or by artificially carbonating it. To be called champagne, it must be made using the prescribed method and be produced in the Champagne region of France, a region about 100 miles (160 km) northeast of Paris around the towns of Rheims and Epernay. Champagne cocktails are not only elegant and delicious, but are a very good way of extending this king of wines among more thirsty revellers! Once again, if you want to add sparkle, but are on a budget, there are many fine sparkling wines, *vins moussex*, available to choose from.

Juices and Mixers

In addition to your selected spirits, liqueurs, fortified wines and champagne, a well-stocked bar needs fresh fruit juices, and 'mixers' such as cola, lemonade, ginger ale, tonic and soda water. Like your spirituous ingredients, buy the best quality for the best tastes and flavours. If you can squeeze your own fruit juices, these will be even tastier than juices in cartons or cans, but its a good idea to pass the squeezed fruit juices through a fine sieve to remove any 'pips and bits' that might spoil the finished drink.

The bar staples in this department are lemon (and lime) juice, grenadine, and a simple sugar syrup, sometimes called gomme syrup.

You can squeeze lemons and limes by hand with a reamer, but if you have to make up a quantity, the best way is to peel the fruits, pop them in a blender or food processor and blitz them. Then strain the juice through a very fine sieve to remove any 'impurities'.

Grenadine is a sweet syrup, flavoured with pomegranate juice which gives it a rich, pink colour. It is used to add colour, flavour and sweetness to many cocktails. Grenadine is non-alcoholic – or has a very low alcohol content, so once the bottle is opened, the syrup will being to ferment and mould. Keep it in a cool place – but not in the fridge as this can cause the sugar to crystallise or harden, making it harder to mix with other ingredients. Other non-alcoholic syrups used include pineapple and orgeat (an almond-flavoured syrup). These are widely available because they are used in making ice-cream desserts, 'posh' milkshakes and smoothies! If you don't have any don't worry: a purée of fresh pineapple – mashed and rubbed through a fine sieve to remove lumps – works just as well. In the case of orgeat, you can substitute with an equal measure of amaretto!

A number of drinks call for sweetening to offset the 'tartness' of some juices. Granulated sugar doesn't dissolve that easily in cold 'solutions' so a sugar, or gomme syrup, being liquid – and colourless – is a simple but effective alternative.

To make a sugar/gomme syrup:

Dissolve equal volumes of water and sugar – say 8 oz (200 gms) sugar in 8 fl oz (250 ml) of water – and simmer in a saucepan over a very low heat until all the sugar is dissolved. You may need to 'skim' the syrup to make it clear. Allow the syrup to cool and then decant it into a handy-sized bottle that pours well. Store in a cool place.

Coconut Cream

Some recipes call for coconut cream: you can buy it ready-made in cans, but this is usually for culinary use, for preparing dishes like curry and, until it is cooked with the other ingredients, it tastes pretty disgusting! On the other hand, specially prepared coconut cream made for drinks is usually hyper-sweet and is full of preservatives. It is very easy to make your own:

Take a chilled, hard block of pure creamed coconut and grate it up to break down the grainy texture. Use 1 tablespoon of the grated coconut cream with slightly less than 1 tablespoon of caster sugar (you can adjust the sweetness to suit your own taste) and mix together with the absolute minimum of hot water. Stir until you have a smooth, creamy paste that is slightly runny, but coats the back of a spoon. When it's cool, it's ready for use. Use it the same day: if you try to store it it will separate, become grainy and, worse, turn rancid!

Garnishes

Some cocktails and mixed drinks are served 'unadorned' – without fruit garnishes, straws or stirrers. This will be specified for each recipe. However, fresh fruit garnishes not only add visual excitement but are edible too! If an olive is called for, don't use one stuffed with anchovy unless you want a fish flavour added to your drink! It's a good idea to rinse off olives before you use them so that any excess oil or brine is removed. Garnishes are your golden opportunity to display artistic skill, so be bold and be adventurous and, most of all, enjoy yourself. You can prepare garnishes in advance so that they are ready to be popped into the drink, onto the glass or onto a cocktail stick or speared with other fruits to create a veritable 'Carmen Miranda' hat! Make sure the fruit is fresh and all skins have been washed.

Planning a Party

The recipes offered in this book give measurements sufficient to make ONE drink, unless otherwise specified. If you are planning on serving a number of mixed drinks at a party, use the table below to help you calculate roughly just how many bottles you will need:

How many drinks in a bottle? If you use a measure of 1.5 fl oz (37.5 ml), you can get approximately this number of measures from each of the different size bottles:

1.5 fl oz (37.5 ml) measure							
Bottles	1	2	4	6	8	10	12
27 fl oz (75 cl) measures	16	33	67	101	135	169	203
36 fl oz (1 litre)	22	45	90	135	180	225	270
54 fl oz (1.5 litre)	39	78	157	236	315	394	473

So, two 27 fl oz (75 cl) bottles of whisky will yield you 33 measures (of 1.5 oz/37.5 ml); two x 1 litre bottles of whisky will yield 45 measures and so on.

Cool Classics

While the heyday of the cocktail was from the 1920s though to the 1930s, many of the world's favourite cocktails – the Mint Julep, the Daiquiri, the Gin Fizz, and the famous Martini – were invented long before that time. The first cocktail book was, in fact, published in the 1860s. *The Bon Vivant's Guide or How to Mix Drinks*, it was written by legendary bartender 'Professor' Jerry Thomas. Interest in the fine art of mixing drinks led to other publications soon afterwards: Harry Johnson's *Illustrated Bartender's Manual*, published in 1882 was a landmark in that it featured an illustration of an ice-filled bar glass with an inverted metal cone – the first cocktail shaker.

What really encouraged the development of cocktails – short drinks that provided a quick hit – and changed the drinking habits of America, was the introduction of the Volstead Act on January 17, 1920. The Volstead Act ushered in 'Prohibition': it was now illegal to manufacture, sell, deliver or trade in alcohol. But Prohibition did not stop drinking – it just drove it behind closed doors and created a secret world of smoke and jazz-filled speak-easy clubs, the location of which – and means of entry to – were known to a few. Perhaps it was because of the very fact that alcohol was forbidden that cocktails became so alluring and this is reflected in many of their names, for example, The Temptation, One Exciting Night, and Fallen Angel.

Many of these drinks were designed during the Prohibition years in America to 'cover up' the taste of 'bootlegged' and 'bathtub' spirits and were, no doubt, short in size in case of a raid by the police, so that they could be disposed of very easily!

Since Britain and Continental Europe did not have the same restrictions on alcohol, émigrés and expats in search of a drink could, if able to afford the time and money to take a long sea journey

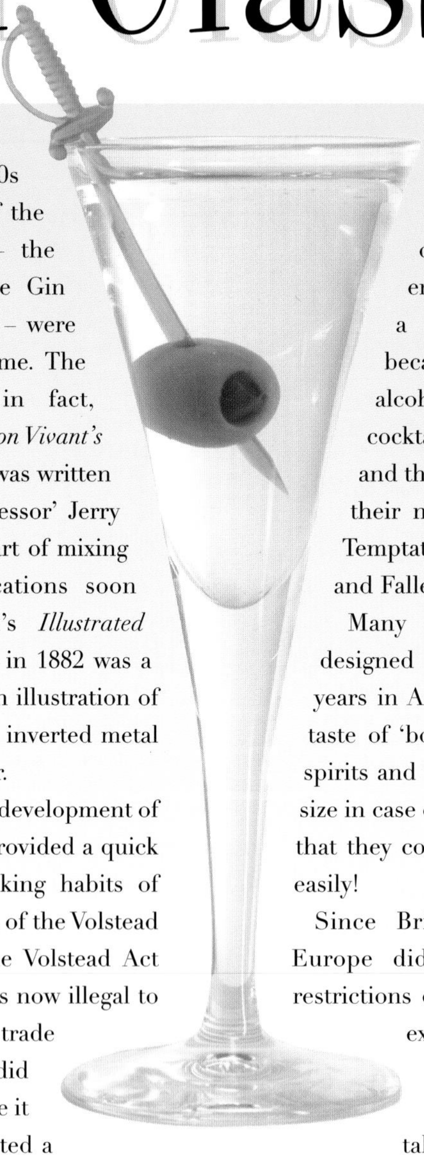

Harry's Cocktail

see page 39.

Caesar Ritz

see page 33.

across the Atlantic, enjoy a huge range of new drinks fashioned with flavours from Europe. Harry's New York Bar at 5 rue Daunou, in Paris – the oldest cocktail bar in Europe – and the American Bar at the Savoy Hotel in London's Strand, were venues for good drinks and good times, and many cocktails bear names that are testimony to their European origins: the RAC Cocktail, Tour de France, London Bus and Palais Royale.

For those who needed to satisfy their thirst more quickly, there were also plenty of exotic locations closer to home: the Caribbean Islands, Mexico and South America all provided escape routes and were great sources of liquors, liqueurs and tropical fruits. Bartending legend Constantino 'Constante' Ribailagua of La Floridita Bar – nicknamed 'La Catedral del Daiquiri' – on the corner of Montserrat Street in Havana, Cuba, was regularly quenching thirsts with his frozen daiquiris and named a cocktail in honour of his regular customer, novelist Ernest Hemingway.

For the most part, the classic cocktails and mixed drinks of this era are based largely on one or more 'base' spirits: gin, vodka, brandy, rum, whisky (in all its guises from rye and bourbon, scotch and Irish, to Canadian and Japanese). Tequila is a relative newcomer to the cocktail scene: while the Margarita is the best known tequila cocktail and was devised in the 1930s, tequila did not have any great impact into the US until the 1960s and was virtually unknown in Europe until the 1970s.

To these 'base' spirits, legendary bartenders like Harry Craddock, Harry MacElhone, Robert Vermeire at the RAC Club in London, and Ngiam Tong Boon at the Raffles Hotel in Singapore, Don Beach and Victor 'Trader Vic' Bergeron, would create not only exciting drinks, but keep the cocktail alive with their inventive approach and create landmarks in the cultural history of the 20th century.

method:	SHAKER
glass:	COCKTAIL OR OLD-FASHIONED

Beauty Cocktail

Devised originally by Harry MacElhone of Harry's New York Bar at 5 rue Daunou, Paris.

Method:

Shake all the ingredients except the port in a shaker with some cracked ice. Shake and strain into a cocktail glass and top with the port. If served in an old-fashioned glass, decorate with a sprig of mint and serve with short straws.

Ingredients:

- ¾ measure brandy
- ¾ measure dry vermouth
- ¾ measure orange juice
- ¼ measure white creme de menthe
- 1 dash grenadine
- 1 dash – or more – port

method:	BUILD OR SHAKE
glass:	COCKTAIL, OLD-FASHIONED OR HIGHBALL

Black Russian

Originally, this drink was served as a short drink – either on the rocks or shaken and strained. In the 1950s, cola was added to make a long drink and a more popular version. Try one either way.

Ingredients:

1½ measures vodka
1 measure Tia Maria
(cold cola if long version is desired)

Method:

Shaker: place ingredients in shaker with two or three ice cubes. Shake and strain into cocktail glass.

Build (short): Fill an old-fashioned glass two-thirds full with ice cubes, pour in vodka, then the Tia Maria and stir.

Build (long): Fill a highball glass with ice cubes and pour in the vodka, the Tia Maria and top with cold cola. Serve with straws.

Block and Fall Cocktail

This recipe was devised in 1924 at Deauville, France – famous for its casino and horse races – by T. Van Dycke from Ciro's Club.

Ingredients:

1 measure Cognac
1 measure Cointreau
½ measure Calvados
½ measure anis (substitute: Pernod)

Method:

Place the ingredients in a shaker with some ice cubes and shake well. Strain and pour into a cocktail glass.

Bunny Hug

The Bunny Hug was a risqué, but popular dance in the 1920s danced to a syncopated rhythm – a 'bunny' was a euphemism for a 'bottom'!

Ingredients:

1 measure gin
1 measure Scotch whisky
1 measure Pernod or Ricard

Method:

Place all the ingredients in a shaker along with some ice cubes and shake well. Strain into a chilled cocktail glass.

method:	SHAKER
glass:	COCKTAIL

Lady be Good

But be just a little wicked too!

Ingredients:

1½ measures brandy

½ measure white creme de menthe

½ measure sweet vermouth

Method:

Place all the ingredients in a shaker with some ice cubes. Shake and strain into a cocktail glass.

method:	MIXING GLASS
glass:	COCKTAIL
garnish:	CHERRY SOAKED IN KIRSCH

Caesar Ritz

A subtle fruit-flavoured cocktail created at the Hotel Ritz in Paris that uses a touch of kirsch – a colourless 'eau de vie' (white brandy) distilled from black cherries and their stones.

Ingredients:

2 measures gin
⅔ measure dry vermouth
⅓ measure cherry brandy
⅓ measure Kirsch

Method:

Place all the liquors into a mixing glass with some ice cubes and stir well. Strain into a chilled cocktail glass and garnish with the Kirsch-soaked red cherry.

method:	MIXING GLASS (NOS. 1 AND 3) SHAKER (NO. 2)
glass:	COCKTAIL

Corpse Reviver

The wonderfully inspired Corpse Reviver was created by Frank Meier at the Ritz Bar in Paris in the 1920s. The Savoy Cocktail Book *stated that it should be drunk "before 11 am, or whenever steam and energy are needed"! Harry Craddock maintained that four Corpse Revivers No. 2., drunk one after the other, would 'un–revive the corpse'. The No. 2 calls for Lillet, a dry, light vermouth from France with a slight orange tinge, while The Corpse Reviver No. 3, the creation of Johnny Johnson of the Savoy in 1948, traditionally uses Fernet-Branca, an Italian bitter often recommended as a hangover cure!*

Method:

No. 1:

Pour the ingredients into a mixing glass with ice cubes and stir. Strain into a cocktail glass.

Ingredients:

Corpse Reviver No. 1:

1 measure brandy

⅔ measure sweet vermouth

⅔ measure Calvados

Corpse Reviver No. 2:

½ measure lemon juice

½ measure Lillet

½ measure Cointreau

½ measure gin

1 dash Pernod

Corpse Reviver No. 3:

1 measure brandy

1 measure white creme de menthe

1 measure Fernet-Branca

Method:

No. 2:

Place all the ingredients in a shaker with some ice cubes and shake sharply. Strain into a cocktail glass.

Cool Classics

Method:

No. 3:

Pour the ingredients into a mixing glass with ice and stir well. Strain into a cocktail glass.

method: SHAKER
glass: OLD-FASHIONED

Dempsey

Many cocktails were created to mark special events and outstanding achievements. The Dempsey was devised in 1921 to celebrate boxer Jack Dempsey's world championship victory.

Ingredients:

1 measure gin
1 measure Calvados
½ teaspoon Pernod
½ teaspoon grenadine

Method:

Place all the ingredients in a shaker with some ice cubes and shake well. Strain into an old-fashioned glass filled three-quarters with broken ice.

method:	MIXING GLASS
glass:	CHAMPAGNE SAUCER

Gloom Raiser

Devised in 1915 by Robert Vermeire at the Royal Automobile Club, Pall Mall, London, the Gloom Raiser was no doubt intended to raise the spirits during World War I.

Ingredients:

2 measures gin
1 measure Noilly Prat (dry vermouth)
1 teaspoon Pernod
1 teaspoon grenadine
1 twist of lemon

Method:

Place all the ingredients in a mixing glass with some ice cubes and stir. Strain into a champagne saucer, squeeze on the lemon twist and discard.

method:	BUILD
glass:	GOBLET OR OVERSIZED GOBLET (LONG FALL), COCKTAIL (SHORT FALL)
garnish:	SLICE OF LIME

Fallen Angel

How far you want to fall is up to you: 'long' or 'short' are both delicious descents.

Method:

To a goblet or oversized wine glass filled three quarters with broken ice, add the ingredients and top with lemonade. Garnish with a slice of lime and serve with straws.

For a 'short fall', add ½ measure of sugar syrup, shake with ice cubes in a shaker, strain into an ice-filled glass and omit the lemonade.

Ingredients:

1½ measure gin
1 measure lime juice
1 teaspoon white creme de menthe
1 dash angostura bitters
4 measures lemonade

method:	SHAKER
glass:	COCKTAIL
garnish:	STUFFED OLIVE

Harry's Cocktail

Created in 1910 by the great Harry MacElhone at the Casino Bar, Aix-les-Bains, France.

Ingredients:

⅔ measure gin
⅓ measure sweet vermouth
1 dash absinthe (substitute: Pernod or Ricard)
2 sprigs of mint

Method:

Shake all the ingredients in a shaker with some ice cubes. Strain into a chilled cocktail glass and serve with a stuffed olive.

method:	SHAKER
glass:	COLLINS
garnish:	MINT SPRIG & SPENT LIME SHELL

Mai Tai

Victor 'Trader Vic' Bergeron (1901–91) was one of the most creative restaurateurs of the 20th century and became famous for his combinations of exotic foods and tropically inspired drinks. In 1944 Trader Vic invented the Mai Tai – Tahitian for 'the best' – using the finest ingredients he could find: a mix of 17-year-old J. Wray & Nephew rum, triple sec, orgeat (a non-alcoholic almond-flavoured syrup), sugar syrup and lime juice. When the Mai Tai was introduced to Hawaii in 1953, it was so popular that, within a year, all the stocks of 17-year-old rum in the world were exhausted, and the cocktail had to be reinvented using a blend of rums. What follows is the 'standard' bar recipe for a classic Mai Tai.

Method:

Place all the ingredients into a shaker with a glass of crushed ice and shake briefly. Pour into the collins glass. Add the spent lime shell and garnish with the mint sprig. Serve with a straw and a stirrer.

Ingredients:

1 measure white rum
1 measure dark rum
⅔ measure triple sec/Cointreau
⅓ measure orgeat (substitute: amaretto)
⅓ measure sugar syrup
¼ measure grenadine
juice of 1 lime

method:	BUILD
glass:	OLD-FASHIONED
garnish:	TWIST OF LEMON

Vanderbilt

This cocktail was devised by 'Guido' of the Kursaal Bar in Ostend, Belgium, in 1912 to mark the visit of American millionaire, Colonel Corneluis Vanderbilt. Shortly afterwards the Colonel drowned when the Lusitania was sunk, and the cocktail became internationally famous.

Ingredients:

1½ measures cognac
1 measure cherry brandy
1 teaspoon sugar syrup
1 dash angostura bitters

Method:

Into an old fashioned glass filled with broken ice, add the ingredients. Add the lemon twist.

method:	BUILD
glass:	OLD-FASHIONED

Sazerac

The Sazerac is a cocktail that made its film debut alongside James Bond in Live and Let Die. *You can buy ready-mixed Sazerac, but here's how to make it yourself.*

Ingredients:

4 dashes anis (substitute: Pernod)
1 white sugar cube
4 dashes of angostura bitters
1 small dash soda water
2 measures bourbon

Method:

Coat the inside of an old-fashioned glass with the 4 dashes of anis/Pernod. Place the sugar cube onto a long-handled bar spoon and coat with the angostura bitters. Place the soaked sugar in the bottom of the glass and add a very small dash of soda water. Crush the sugar cube with the back of the bar spoon. Fill the glass two-thirds full with cracked ice and pour in the bourbon. Serve with a stirrer.

Scoff Law Cocktail

This cocktail was devised in 1924 by Jock, the bartender at Harry's Bar in Paris, and was named in honour of all those Americans who were intent on dodging Prohibition.

Ingredients:

1 measure Canadian whisky
1 measure dry vermouth
½ measure lemon juice
½ measure grenadine

Method:

Place all the ingredients in a shaker with some ice cubes. Shake well and strain into a chilled cocktail glass while turning a blind eye!

method:	MIXING GLASS
glass:	COCKTAIL
garnish:	CHERRY ON A STICK, ORANGE TWIST

RAC Cocktail

The Royal Automobile Club premises in Pall Mall, London, (1908–11) were designed by Arthur J. Davis and Charles Mewes and include a fabulous neo-classical swimming pool. Along with the Ritz Hotel in London, also designed by Davis and Mewes, these buildings, and their sumptuous interiors, are among the jewels of Edwardian architecture. The RAC Cocktail is also a jewel, created in 1914 by Fred Faecks at the RAC.

Method:

Place all the ingredients in a mixing glass with some ice cubes. Stir and strain into a cocktail glass and add a cherry on a stick. Squeeze a twist of orange over the drink and discard.

Ingredients:

1½ measures gin
¾ measure dry vermouth
¾ measure rosso vermouth
1 teaspoon orange bitters (Substitute: dry orange Curaçao)
1 teaspoon grenadine

Prohibition Cocktail

The Volstead Act prohibiting the manufacture, distribution and sale of alcohol led to a hugely inventive period in cocktail making – largely because the bootlegged liquor was so awful it had to be mixed to disguise the taste! Why not try this out on December 5 – the day in 1933 that saw the end of Prohibition.

Ingredients:

2 measures gin
2 measures Lillet (dry vermouth)
½ teaspoon apricot brandy
1 teaspoon orange juice

Method:

While you whistle *Happy Days Are Here Again*, place all the ingredients in a shaker with ice cubes and shake well. Strain into a cocktail glass, squeeze over a twist of lemon and discard.

method:	SHAKER
glass:	COCKTAIL
garnish:	SLICE OF ORANGE WRAPPED AROUND A CHERRY

Monkey's Gland Cocktail

This strangely named cocktail was devised by Harry MacElhone around 1920 – at the time when Dr. Serge Voronoff was experimenting with injections of all manner of ingredients which aimed to stop the ageing process! A simpler, and more effective solution is to be found in Harry's rejuvenating elixir.

Ingredients:

2 measures gin
2 measures orange juice
1 teaspoon Pernod
2 teaspoons grenadine

Method:

Place all the ingredients in a shaker with ice cubes and shake well. Strain into a cocktail glass and garnish with the cherry wrapped in the slice of orange. Feel younger instantly.

method:	SHAKER
glass:	LARGE COCKTAIL
garnish:	CHERRY ON A STICK

Mary Pickford

This drink was created for the Hollywood movie actress, Mary Pickford, in the 1920s at the Hotel Sevilla Bar, Cuba.

Ingredients:

1½ measures white rum
1 teaspoon maraschino
1½ measures pineapple juice
1 teaspoon grenadine

Method:

Place all the ingredients in a shaker and shake well. Strain into a large cocktail glass filled with crushed ice. Add the cherry on a stick and serve with short straws.

method:	BUILD
glass:	HIGHBALL
garnish:	SLICE OF PINEAPPLE AND A CHERRY

Singapore Sling

The world famous Singapore Sling was devised at the Raffles Hotel in Singapore, in 1915, by Ngiam Tong Boon. It was originally intended as a 'lady's drink', but it soon became widely enjoyed by both sexes. It was the favourite drink of writers Somerset Maugham, Joseph Conrad and Hollywood actor Douglas Fairbanks. Some 'modern' interpretations use soda water to finish the drink but in this, the Raffles Hotel version, it is never used. Where possible, use a very brightly coloured cherry brandy so the resulting drink is a beautiful pink colour.

Method:

Place all the ingredients except the Benedictine into a shaker with ice cubes and shake well. Strain into a highball glass filled three-quarters with broken ice and sprinkle the Benedictine on top. Garnish with the slice of pineapple and the cherry.

Ingredients:

1 measure gin
1 measure cherry brandy
½ measure Cointreau
1 measure lime juice
1 measure pineapple juice
1 measure orange juice
¼ measure grenadine
1 teaspoon Benedictine
1 dash angostura bitters

Caruso

This minty cocktail was invented and named after the great Italian tenor, Enrico Caruso, when he stayed at the Hotel Sevilla, Cuba in the 1920s.

Ingredients:

- 1 measure gin
- 1 measure dry vermouth
- 1 measure green creme de menthe

Method:

In a mixing glass with some ice cubes, stir in the ingredients and strain into a cocktail glass.

If you use white creme de menthe in place of the green, you have a Caruso Blanco.

method: SHAKER
glass: COCKTAIL

Bosom Caresser

A naughty – but very nice – cocktail from the Prohibition era.

Method:

Place all the ingredients in a shaker with some ice cubes and shake vigourously. Strain into a cocktail glass.

Ingredients:

1 measure Madeira
¾ measure brandy
½ measure triple sec/Cointreau
1 teaspoon grenadine
1 egg yolk

Stinger

Simple – yet very effective.

Ingredients:

1½ measures brandy

½ measure white creme de menthe

Method:

Add some ice to a shaker and pour in the brandy and creme de menthe. Shake well and strain into a cocktail glass.

method:	SHAKER
glass:	COCKTAIL
garnish:	CHERRY

Casino

For the man 'who broke the bank at Monte Carlo'.

Method:

Place all the ingredients into a shaker with some ice cubes and shake well. Strain into a cocktail glass and add the cherry.

Ingredients:

2 dashes orange bitters
¼ teaspoon maraschino
¼ teaspoon lemon juice
2 measures gin

Angel Face

More an angel with a dirty face!

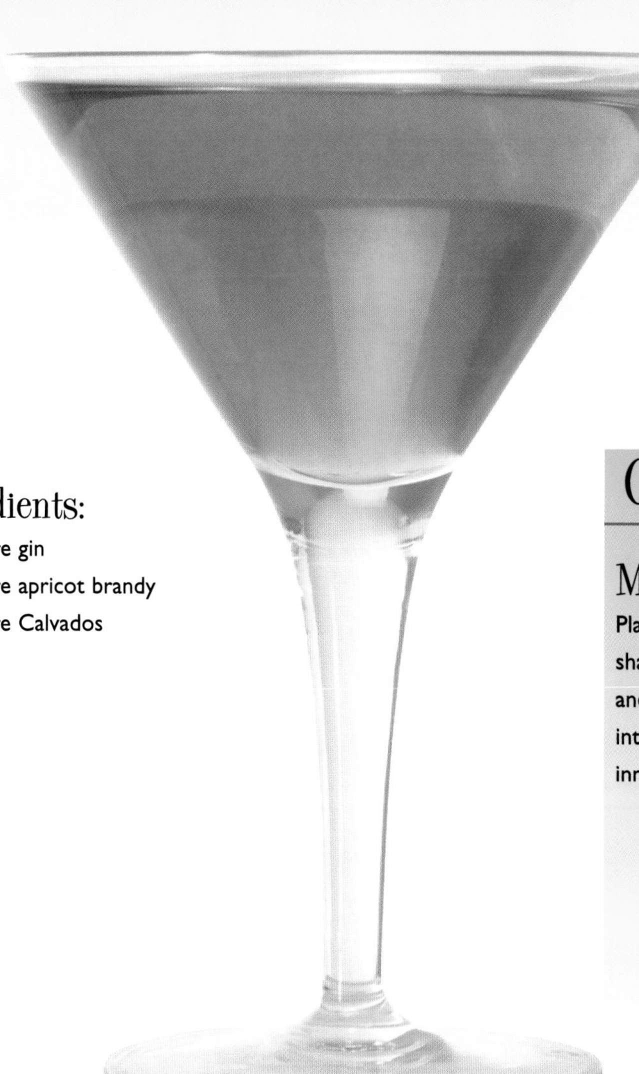

Ingredients:

1 measure gin
1 measure apricot brandy
1 measure Calvados

Method:

Place all the ingredients in a shaker with some ice cubes and shake vigourously. Strain into a cocktail glass and look innocent!

method:	SHAKER
glass:	HIGHBALL
garnish:	SPRIG OF MINT, SLICES OF LIME AND PINEAPPLE

Zombie

This incredible rum drink was invented in 1934 by Don Beach at Don the Beachcomber Restaurant in Hollywood, California. Bar-lore tells how Don Beach produced this drink for a guest who, suffering from a hangover, said he felt like a zombie. This is just one of Don Beach's 63 exotic cocktail recipes where, it appears, the aim was to get as much alcohol in one glass as possible! If you don't feel like a zombie before, you may just well feel like one afterwards!

Method:

Place all the ingredients except the over-proof dark rum in a shaker with a glass worth of crushed ice. Shake briefly and strain into a highball glass filled with crushed ice. Garnish with a sprig of mint and slices of lime and pineapple. Add straws and dribble the over-proof dark rum on top with a long-handled bar spoon.

Ingredients:

½ measure light rum
1 measure golden rum
½ measure dark rum
½ measure cherry brandy
½ measure apricot brandy
2 measures pineapple juice
1 measure orange juice
¾ measure lime juice
½ measure papaya juice
¼ measure orgeat
⅓ measure over-proof dark rum

White Lady Cocktail

This is the original recipe by Harry MacElhone created at Ciro's Club, in London, in 1919. Harry later changed the recipe in 1929 at his own bar in Paris, replacing the white creme de menthe with gin.

Ingredients:

I measure lemon juice
I measure white creme de menthe
I measure Cointreau

Method:

Place the ingredients in a shaker with some ice cubes and shake well. Strain into a cocktail glass.

method:	SHAKER
glass:	CHAMPAGNE SAUCER

Clover Club

This rich lemon-flavoured cocktail burst onto the scene in 1925 and takes it name from the famous American night-spot.

Ingredients:

1½ measures gin
¾ measure lemon juice
½ measure grenadine
1 egg white

Variations

Add 4 to 5 mint leaves to the shaker and garnish with a sprig of mint and you have a Clover Leaf.

For a Clover Club Royal, reduce the grenadine to ¼ measure and replace the egg white with an egg yolk. Shake well and strain into a double Champagne saucer filled with crushed ice and garnish with a slice of lemon.

Method:

Place all the ingredients in a shaker with some ice cubes and shake vigourously. Strain into a champagne saucer.

Exotics

Travel and tourism over the past one hundred years have opened peoples' eyes to the lands, traditions and cultures of many parts of the world that were once inaccessible to most ordinary people. We also discovered new flavours and new foods that tantalised our taste buds. Exciting new drinks and new ingredients like tequila burst on to the scene as travellers ventured to Central and South America, the Pacific, Australasia and Southeast Asia. But even the 'old' cocktail staples like gin, vodka, brandy and rum became more exciting as we discovered the subtle variations in flavours and unique tastes of the same spirits made in other countries.

The invention of rum dates from the establishment of sugar plantations in the West Indies in the early 16th century. The rough spirit that was first produced as a by-product of the sugar industry was described as 'hot, hellish and terrible'! But, as new techniques were developed, the spirit became infinitely more palatable.

Bali Punch

see page 65.

Today rum is produced all over the West Indies and Eastern South America, in the Indian Ocean – the Philippines and Mauritius – as well as in small quantities in the USA and Australia. Rum is distilled from molasses and, in some cases, for example as with Aguardente de Cana, commonly known as 'cachaca', directly from the fermented sap of sugar cane. There are basically three types of rum: white, golden and dark. All three, however, begin as a colourless spirit to which caramel may be added to give colour, while others acquire their colour from being aged, sometimes for decades, in oak casks. White rum, the best-known brand of which is Bacardi, made in the Bahamas, is the biggest selling of all the rums. Other fine white rums come from Martinique (Rhum St. James) which has a different flavour, described as more of a 'burnt-sugar' flavour. The classic formula for a rum punch in Martinque is the beautifully singsong: 'One of sour, two of sweet, three of strong and four of weak'. Order a rum punch here and you'll be given a slice of lime (sour), some sugar syrup (sweet), a bottle of rum (strong) and a jug of water (weak) and left to mix it yourself!

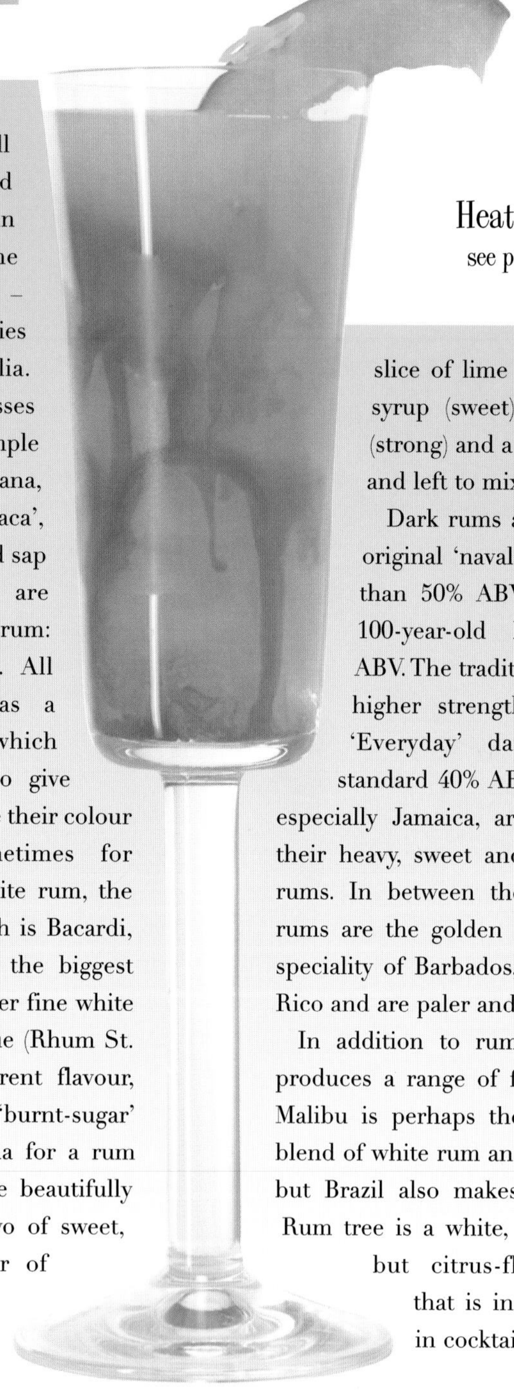

Heat Wave
see page 83.

Dark rums are bottled at their original 'naval' strength of more than 50% ABV, such as Wood's 100-year-old Navy Rum at 57% ABV. The traditional name for this higher strength is 'over proof'. 'Everyday' dark rums are a standard 40% ABV: Martinique and especially Jamaica, are well known for their heavy, sweet and full-bodied dark rums. In between the white and dark rums are the golden rums. These are a speciality of Barbados, Cuba and Puerto Rico and are paler and drier.

In addition to rum, the region also produces a range of flavoured liqueurs: Malibu is perhaps the best known – a blend of white rum and coconut extracts, but Brazil also makes Batida de Coco. Rum tree is a white, rum-based, sweet, but citrus-flavoured, liqueur that is increasingly popular in cocktail recipes.

The tradition of drinking fiery spirits in Central and South America stems from the early Spanish colonists who planted the first vines. In addition to producing wines, fiery brandies were also made. Mexico produces one called Presidente, but an interesting contribution is pisco, a colourless brandy distilled in Peru, Chile and Bolivia.

From Mexico come mescal and tequila. Mescal is a pale yellowish spirit made from the fermented juice of the agave cactus and is often sold with a pickled white agave worm in the bottom. This is real and is intended for eating as the last of the mescal is poured from the bottle – if you are brave enough. Mescal is the first rough distillation of the pulque (the pressed cactus juice), and is not therefore, a very 'sophisticated' product: it does not blend well with anything beyond lime juice and the mescal worm! Tequila is one stage down the line to refinement: the pulque is distilled twice and then cask aged. It comes in two versions: silver (clear) and gold (oro) and the two brands most commonly encountered are Cuervo and Montezuma.

Other famous products from the new world include kahlua a dark brown, coffee-flavoured liqueur from Mexico.

Japanese Slipper

see page 72.

Mustique Whammy
see page 69.

Kahlua is slightly thicker in texture, but a little less sweet than it's famous rival, Tia Maria which, in spite of it's Italian-sounding name, in fact comes from Jamaica.

Tropical fruits, either in their 'natural state' as juices or added to a spirit base to make liqueurs, have long been the way to make exotic-flavoured cocktails: orange-flavoured Curaçaos, grenadine (a sweet, red low or non-alcoholic cordial made from pomegranates) and creme liqueurs are staples of the cocktail bar. Some more recent additions come from Indonesia, Japan and Hawaii: pisang ambon is a green banana and herb flavoured liqueur. Ambon is the name of an Indonesian island, where '*pisang*' means 'banana'. Sake is Japanese rice beer. Traditionally served warm when neat, it is now appearing in many new cocktails, while okelehao, is a spirit distilled in Hawaii from the mashed and fermented root of the ti plant.

The range of ingredients on offer have inspired bartenders across the world to invent exciting new combinations, and such is their generosity, many of their recipes are freely available for you to recreate. So relive those tropical sunsets at any time of year and share happy moments with friends and loved ones with these magical drinks.

method:	SHAKER
glass:	COCKTAIL
garnish:	CHERRY AND A SLICE OF ORANGE

Acapulco

Tequila and kahlua from Mexico blended with rum and coconut from the Caribbean in a drink to make you bold enough to make the famous high dive into the Pacific Ocean!

Ingredients:

1 measure gold tequila
1 measure kahlua
⅔ measure dark rum
½ measure coconut cream

Method:

Shake all the ingredients together in a shaker with some ice cubes. Shake well and strain into a cocktail glass and garnish with the orange slice and the cherry.

method:	SHAKER
glass:	HIGHBALL
garnish:	CHERRY AND ORANGE PEEL SPIRAL

St. Lucia

One to recall the tropical paradise of the beautiful island of St. Lucia.

Ingredients:

2 measures white or golden rum
1 measure dry vermouth
1 measure Curaçao
juice of ½ orange
1 teaspoon grenadine

Method:

Place the ingredients in a shaker with some ice cubes and shake vigourously. Pour, without straining, into a highball glass and decorate with the orange peel spiral and the cherry.

method:	SHAKER
glass:	OLD-FASHIONED
garnish:	FRUIT IN SEASON

Tequila Exotica

Ingredients:

1½ measures gold tequila

¼ measure white creme de cacao

1 teaspoon triple sec/Cointreau

1 measure mango juice

1 measure white grape juice

½ measure lime juice

Method:

Place all the ingredients, except the garnish, into a cocktail shaker with some ice cubes. Shake and strain into an old-fashioned glass filled two-thirds with broken ice. Garnish with seasonal fruit and serve with straws.

method:	SHAKER
glass:	COCKTAIL
garnish:	VERY THIN SLICE OF LEMON

Bahamas

A peachy-banana delight.

Method:

Put some ice cubes in the shaker, pour in the ingredients and shake well. Strain into a chilled cocktail glass and drop in a very thin slice of lemon.

Ingredients:

1 measure white rum
1 measure Southern Comfort
1 measure lemon juice
1 dash creme de banane

method:	SHAKER
glass:	COLLINS
garnish:	FRUIT IN SEASON

Bali Punch

Ingredients:

1½ measures white rum
½ measure coconut rum (such as Malibu or Batida de Coco)
1 measure lime juice
2 measures passion fruit juice
2 measures orangeade
½ measure pineapple syrup

Method:

Place all the ingredients except the orangeade into a shaker with some ice cubes. Shake well and strain into an ice-filled collins glass. Add the orangeade and garnish with fruit in season. Serve with straws. Sarong optional!

method: BUILD
glass: OLD-FASHIONED

Ti Punch

This lime-flavoured drink is a traditional aperitif on the French-speaking islands of the Caribbean.

Ingredients:

1 whole lime
2 measures white rum
1 measure sugar syrup

Method:

Wash the lime, top and tail and slice thinly. Put the lime slices into the old-fashioned glass and, with the flat end of a bar spoon, crush them to release the juice. Pour in the rum and sugar syrup and top up with broken ice. Muddle together, add short straws and serve. *A vôtre santé, cher!*

method:	SHAKER
glass:	OLD-FASHIONED AND A SHOT GLASS
garnish:	LIME WEDGE

Pink Cadillac Convertible

A wonderful name for a fun drink.

Ingredients:

4 lime wedges
sea salt
1¼ measures gold tequila
½ measure Cointreau
¾ measure lime juice
¾ measure cranberry juice
¾ measure Grand Marnier

Method:

Rub one of the lime wedges around the rim of an old-fashioned glass, then dip the rim into some sea salt. Fill the glass two-thirds full with ice cubes. Into the cocktail shaker with some ice cubes, squeeze the juice from 2 lime wedges. Press the lime rind to release the oil and then drop the spent shells into the shaker. Pour the tequila, Cointreau, lime juice and cranberry juice into the shaker and shake vigourously. Strain into the ice-filled old-fashion glass and garnish with the remaining lime wedge. Pour the Grand Marnier into a shot glass and serve along side: just before drinking, the Grand Marnier is poured on top of the cocktail.

method: SHAKER

glass: COCKTAIL

Mulata

This lime-flavoured cocktail was created in the 1940s by Cuban barman extraordinaire, Jose Maria Vazquez.

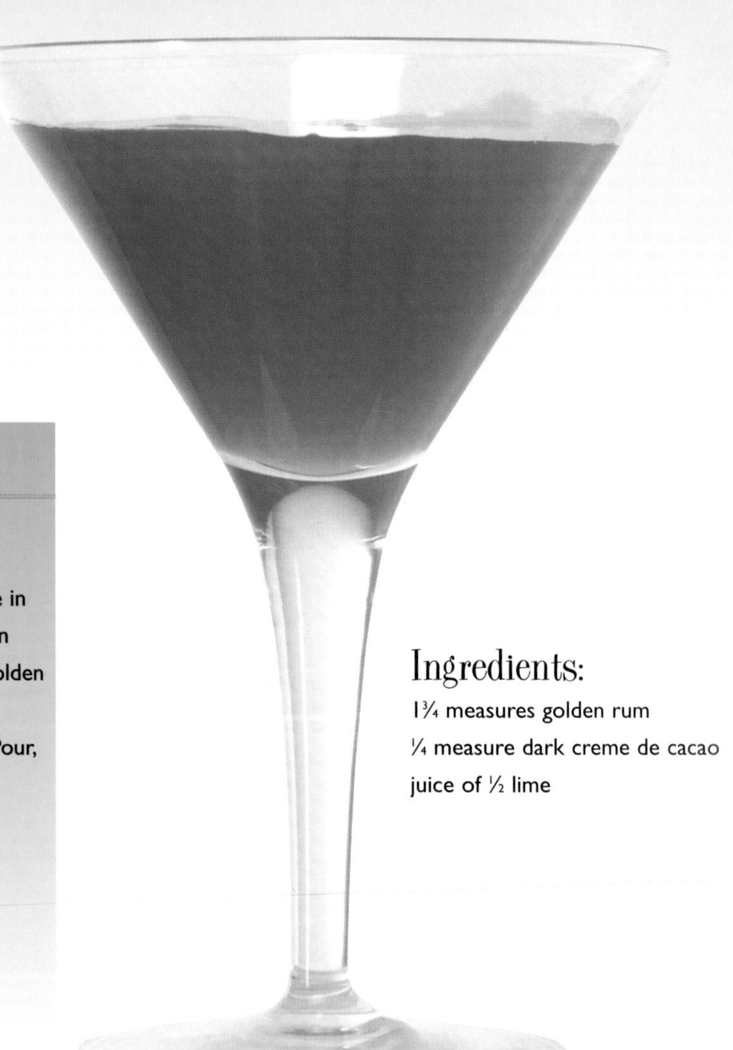

Method:

Put a glass of crushed ice in the shaker and squeeze in the lime juice. Add the golden rum and dark creme de cacao and shake briefly. Pour, unstrained, into a large cocktail glass.

Ingredients:

1¾ measures golden rum
¼ measure dark creme de cacao
juice of ½ lime

Mustique Whammy

From the hideaway of the rich and famous, the Mustique Whammy features Champagne – naturally, darling!

Ingredients:

1 measure golden rum
1 measure orange juice
½ measure lemon juice
¼ measure grenadine
3½ measures well-chilled champagne

Method:

Place all the ingredients, except the champagne, into a shaker with some ice cubes and shake until a froth forms. Strain into a wine glass and pour in the chilled champagne.

method:	SHAKER
glass:	COLLINS
garnish:	COLOURFUL SEASONAL FRUIT

Pisang Garuda

The mythical Garuda – part human, part bird – from ancient Hindu Sanskrit tales is the national emblem of Indonesia, from which comes the green banana liqueur pisang ambon used in this recipe. Because it uses green bananas, pisang ambon has a somewhat different taste to other creme de bananes. But if you don't have any of the Indonesian variety, one of the less sweet creme liqueurs is equally delicious. Mandarine Napoleon is another type of Curaçao, this time made with the skins of Sicilian tangerines as opposed to the bitter Caribbean oranges, and is coloured with carotene to create the vivid yellow colour. Again, at a pinch, if you don't have any of this liquid gold to hand, you can substitute it with Grand Marnier.

Method:

Rim the collins glass with grenadine and then dip into some caster sugar. Fill the glass with ice cubes. Place the ingredients – except the bitter lemon – into a shaker with some ice cubes and shake well. Strain into the ice-filled collins glass and add the bitter lemon. Decorate with seasonal fruit and serve with straws.

Ingredients:

1½ measures pisang ambon (Substitute: creme de banane)
1 measure white rum
½ measure Mandarine Napoleon (substitute: Grand Marnier)
4 measures sparkling bitter lemon

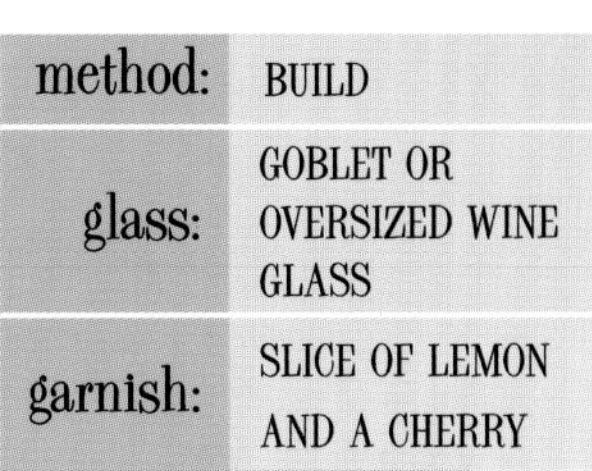

method:	BUILD
glass:	GOBLET OR OVERSIZED WINE GLASS
garnish:	SLICE OF LEMON AND A CHERRY

Stratocaster

A delightful, refreshing fruit-flavoured rum-based drink that's out of this world.

Ingredients:

I measure dark rum
I measure creme de cassis
I teaspoon lemon juice
I measure lemonade
I measure soda water

Method:

Fill a goblet or oversized wine glass with broken ice. Pour in the rum, cassis, lemon juice, lemonade and soda water. Garnish with a slice of lemon and a cherry, and serve with short straws.

method:	SHAKER
glass:	CHAMPAGNE SAUCER
garnish:	SLICE OF LEMON

Japanese Slipper

'Kampai!' – *the traditional Japanese toast.*

Method:

Place all the ingredients in a shaker with some ice cubes and shake well. Strain into a champagne saucer and garnish with a slice of lemon.

Ingredients:

1⅓ measures vodka
1⅓ measures Midori melon liqueur
¾ measure lemon juice

method:	SHAKER
glass:	COLLINS
garnish:	CHERRY, SLICES OF PINEAPPLE AND LEMON

Coconut Grove

One recipe to remember when you're cast away on a topical island!

Ingredients:

1½ measures coconut rum (Malibu or Batida de Coco)
1 measure creme de banane
1 measure white rum
4 measures pineapple juice
1 teaspoon lemon juice

Method:

Place all the ingredients in a shaker with some ice cubes and shake well. Strain into an ice-filled collins glass. Decorate with the cherry and slices of lemon and pineapple. Wait patiently for rescue!

method:	SHAKER
glass:	CHAMPAGNE SAUCER

Cafe Trinidad

The perfect way to end a perfect day.

Ingredients:

1 measure dark rum – preferably Trinidad rum
¾ measure amaretto
¾ measure Tia Maria
1 measure double cream

Method:

Place all the ingredients in a shaker with some ice cubes and shake well. Strain into a champagne saucer.

method:	SHAKER
glass:	COCKTAIL
garnish:	SPIRAL OF LEMON PEEL

Mezcarita

If you do happen to have some mescal, here's a way to enjoy it without having to eat the worm! If not, gold tequila makes a very palatable substitute.

Ingredients:

1½ measures mescal (or gold tequila)
¾ measure Cointreau
1¼ measures lemon juice
salt (chilli salt makes a spicy change!)

Method:

Dampen the rim of the cocktail glass with a little lemon juice and dip into the salt. Add the mescal, Cointreau and lemon juice to a shaker with some ice cubes and shake well. Strain into the cocktail class and decorate with a spiral of lemon peel.

method:	BUILD
glass:	PINA COLADA, HURRICANE OR OVERSIZED WINE GLASS
garnish:	MINT SPRIG AND A CHERRY

Tree House

An opportunity to use rum tree, the white-rum-based citrus-flavoured liqueur.

Ingredients:

1½ measures rum tree

1 measure gold tequila

1 measure grapefruit juice

1 measure pineapple juice

4 measures sparkling bitter lemon

Method:

Fill a piña colada, hurricane or oversized wine glass two-thirds full with ice. Pour in the ingredients, finishing with the sparkling bitter lemon. Garnish with the sprig of mint and the cherry and serve with straws.

method: SHAKER

glass: COCKTAIL

Caribbean Harvest

A medley of tropical fruit flavours in one glass.

Ingredients:

1 measure white rum
1 measure coconut rum
(Malibu or Batida de Coco)
½ measure creme de banane
1 measure passion fruit juice
1 measure mango juice
1 teaspoon grenadine

Exotics

Method:

Place all the ingredients in a shaker with some ice cubes and shake vigourously. Strain into a chilled cocktail glass.

method:	SHAKER
glass:	HIGHBALL
garnish:	MINT SPRIG

Gremlin Fixer

Another very good excuse to use pisang ambon.

Ingredients:

⅔ measure vodka
⅔ measure pisang ambon
(substitute: creme de banane)
⅔ measure dry vermouth
⅓ measure apricot brandy
3 measures pineapple juice

Method:

Place all the ingredients in a shaker with some ice cubes. Shake well and strain into a highball glass filled with crushed ice. Garnish with the mint sprig and serve with straws.

method:	MIXING GLASS
glass:	GOBLET OR OVERSIZED WINE GLASS
garnish:	ORANGE SLICE AND A CHERRY

Wiki Waki Woo

Whacky name, wicked taste!

Ingredients:

½ measure vodka
½ measure white rum
½ measure dark rum (over proof if possible – to provide the 'Woo' bit no doubt!)
½ measure tequila
½ measure triple sec/Cointreau
1 measure amaretto
1 measure orange juice
1 measure pineapple juice
1 measure cranberry juice

Method:

Place all the ingredients in a mixing glass with some ice cubes and stir. Strain into a goblet or oversized wine glass filled two-thirds with broken ice. Garnish with the cherry and the orange slice and serve with straws – and a deck chair.

method:	SHAKER
glass:	HIGHBALL OR COLLINS
garnish:	PINEAPPLE SLICE

Caribbean Cruise

Why limit yourself to one island when you can have them all!

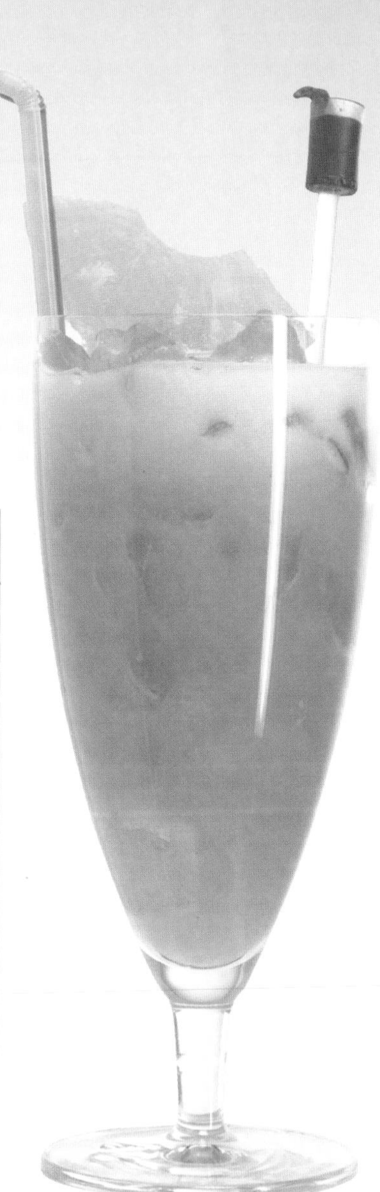

Ingredients:

2 measures vodka
½ measure white rum
½ measure coconut rum
(Malibu or Batida de Coc
2 dashes grenadine
4 measures pineapple juice

Method:

Put some ice cubes into a shaker and pour in the ingredients. Shake well and strain into a highball or Collins glass half-filled with broken ice. Garnish with the pineapple slice and serve with straws.

method:	BUILD
glass:	OLD-FASHIONED

Black Widow

Always remember: the female of the species is more deadly than the male!

Ingredients:

I measure white rum
I measure kahlua

Method:

Fill an old-fashioned glass two-thirds full with broken ice. Pour in the light rum and the kahlua. Serve with a stirrer and a very seductive smile.

method: SHAKER
glass: COLLINS

Marrakech Express

Conjure up memories of the casbah with this luxurious long drink.

Ingredients:

1 measure white rum
1 measure dry vermouth
1 measure white creme de cacao
2 measures grapefruit juice
1 measure mandarin juice
½ measure lime juice
1 level teaspoon caster sugar

Method:

Place all the ingredients in a shaker with a glassful of broken ice and shake well. Pour, unstrained, into a collins glass.

method:	BUILD
glass:	FLUTE
garnish:	PEACH SLICE

Heat Wave

One to be enjoyed anywhere in the world when the sun comes out.

Ingredients:

1¼ measures coconut rum (Malibu or Batido de Coco)
½ measure peach schnapps
3 measures pineapple juice
3 measures orange juice
½ measure grenadine

Method:

Half-fill the flute with finely broken ice and pour in all the ingredients – except the grenadine. Top with the grenadine and garnish with the slice of fresh peach.

method:	SHAKER
glass:	WINE GLASS
garnish:	ORANGE SLICE (OPTIONAL)

Tropical Cocktail

Perfect anywhere!

Ingredients:

I measure dry vermouth
I measure maraschino
I measure white creme de cacao
I dash angostura bitters

Method:

Place all the ingredients in a shaker with plenty of ice and shake vigourously. Strain into a wine glass.

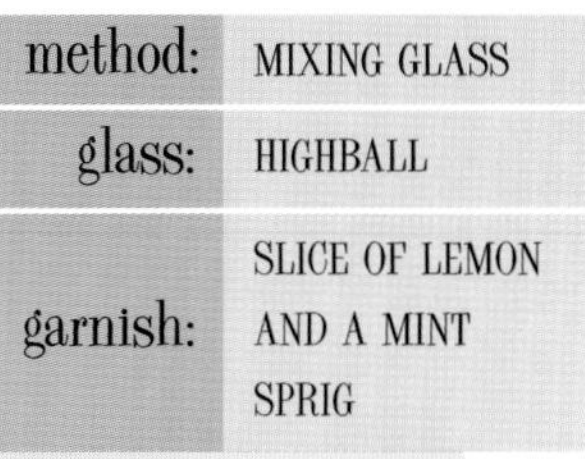

method:	MIXING GLASS
glass:	HIGHBALL
garnish:	SLICE OF LEMON AND A MINT SPRIG

Zombie Christopher

The king of exotic cocktails, Don Beach, created the original Zombie (see page 54) in 1934. Since then a number of equally wonderful variations have appeared including the Zombie Prince and this wonderfully coloured Zombie Christophe.

Ingredients:

juice of 1 lime
juice of ½ orange
250 ml/8 fl oz pineapple juice
1 measure blue Curaçao
1 measure white rum
1 measure golden rum
½ measure dark rum

Exotics

Method:

Put some ice cubes in a mixing glass and squeeze on the lime juice, pressing hard to release the oil from the skin. Pour on the other juices and liquors – except the dark rum – and stir vigourously. Pour, without straining, into a highball glass. Top with the dark rum and stir gently. Garnish with the mint sprig and lemon slice and serve with a stirrer.

method: SHAKER

glass: COCKTAIL

Polynesian Cocktail

The Pacific Ocean islands are divided into three groups: Micronesia (the islands lying north of the equator and east of the Philippines), Melanesia (the islands in the South Pacific, northeast of Australia), and Polynesia (the islands from the Hawaiian Islands south to New Zealand.) One drink alone could not possibly sum up the richness of the culture of these islands – but it's worth trying!

Method:

Moisten the rim of the cocktail glass with a little lime juice and dip into caster sugar. Put some ice cubes in the shaker and squeeze in the lime juice. Pour in the vodka and cherry brandy and shake well. Strain into the prepared cocktail glass.

Ingredients:

juice of 1 lime

1½ measures vodka

¾ measure cherry brandy

method:	SHAKER
glass:	COCKTAIL
garnish:	LEMON TWIST

Bikini

The essential item of clothing for the castaway.

Ingredients:

2 measures vodka
1 measure white rum
½ measure milk
1 teaspoon caster sugar
½ measure lemon juice

Method:

Place all the ingredients in a shaker with ice cubes and shake well. Strain into a chilled cocktail glass.

method:	SHAKER
glass:	COCKTAIL
garnish:	TWO CHERRIES

Lost Bikini

Loose all inhibitions and 'go native'!

Ingredients:

¾ measure Galliano

¾ measure amaretto

½ measure white rum

½ measure lime juice

2 measures mandarin juice

Method:

Place all the ingredients in a shaker with some ice cubes and shake vigourously. Strain into a cocktail glass and garnish with the two cherries.

method:	SHAKER
glass:	COCKTAIL
garnish:	LIME SLICE

Tequila Mockingbird

Raise a glass to Harper Lee.

Ingredients:

1½ measures silver tequila
¾ measure green creme de menthe
½ measure lime juice

Method:

Place all the ingredients in a shaker with some ice cubes and shake well. Strain into a cocktail glass and garnish with lime slices.

method:	SHAKER
glass:	COLLINS

Typhoon

Create a storm with one of these!

Ingredients:

I measure gin
½ measure Pernod or Ricard
I measure lime juice
chilled champagne

Method:

Place all the ingredients, except the champagne, into a shaker with some ice cubes and shake well. Pour into an ice filled collins glass and top up with champagne.

Wakiki Beachcomber

Very simple to make – just three ingredients that washed up on the beach.

Ingredients:

1 measure gin

1 measure triple sec/Cointreau

1½ tablespoons pineapple juice

Method:

Place all the ingredients in a shaker with some ice cubes and shake well. Strain into a cocktail glass.

method:	SHAKER
glass:	OLD-FASHIONED
garnish:	SPRIG OF MINT

Pisco Sour

A chance to try out pisco, a colourless brandy from South America.

Ingredients:

2 measures pisco
juice of ½ lime
1 teaspoon sugar syrup
½ an egg white
1 dash angostura bitters

Method:

Fill an old-fashioned glass with broken ice and, by hand, squeeze in the juice of ½ a lime. Place the remaining ingredients in the shaker with some ice cubes and shake well. Strain into the ice-filled glass and garnish with a sprig of mint.

method:	SHAKER
glass:	HIGHBALL
garnish:	SLICE OF LEMON

Green Caribbean

Ingredients:

1½ measures Midori melon liqueur
1½ measures white rum
soda water

Method:

Place all the ingredients except the soda water into a shaker with some ice cubes and shake well. Strain into an ice-filled highball glass, garnish with a lemon slice and top with soda water.

method:	BUILD
glass:	COLLINS
garnish:	LEMON SLICE AND MINT SPRIG

Oasis

Cool, blue, refreshing – and very quick to make.

Ingredients:

2 measures gin

½ measure blue Curaçao

tonic water

Method:

Fill a collins glass two-thirds full of ice. Pour over the gin and add the Curaçao. Top up with tonic and stir well. Garnish with the lemon slice and mint sprig and serve with a stirrer.

Rich & Elegant

Ritz Fizz
see page 128.

What is a cocktail? Numerous dictionary definitions abound, all of which state pretty much the same thing. In May, 1806, the American magazine *The Balance* offered the following description: 'A cocktail is an intoxicating beverage composed of different spirits, which, mixed with bitters and essences, produce an outstanding drink.' This definition goes beyond all others in the fact that it states that the cocktail is an outstanding drink. This is true, for while it is possible to make delicious drinks from 'ordinary' ingredients, the lasting success of cocktails depends on a well-informed choice of the finest-quality spirits, liqueurs, wines, juices and mixers. Careful – and loving – preparation leads to the production of a 'confection' that is not only infinitely drinkable, but has a particular scent and texture (as opposed to a density) which is the result of the synthesis of the various ingredients.

Distillation (from the Latin *destillare*, meaning 'to drip') is the extraction of higher alcohol from fermented drinks by using the action of heat to vaporise them. Compared to fermentation itself, distillation is a pretty simple process, largely because it is much more readily subject to external control: to produce a fine wine, the weather, the quality of the grape, and the condition of the soil – which can vary from year to year – are largely out of the winemaker's control. Freshly pressed grape juice needs the right ambient temperature to begin the process of turning into wine. A spirit, on the other hand, can be produced from wine simply by adding heat to it. Alcohol has a lower boiling point than water – about 78 °C compared with 100 °C – so alcohol vaporises into steam long before the water content in wine starts to boil. When this alcohol-rich steam hits a cool surface, it forms a dripping condensation and reverts to a liquid form in which the alcohol is of a higher proportion than it was when it was part of the wine. Boil that liquid up again, and the same procedure will yield an ever higher alcohol!

Horn of Plenty
see page 136.

The facts of the early production of alcoholic drinks are lost in the mists of time: centuries of experimentation were needed before the first still was invented: The Greek philosopher, Aristotle, who lived in the 4th century BC wrote of distillation as a method of purifying sea water to make it drinkable. But it was not until around 1100 AD – in Europe at least – at the famous medical school in Salerno, Italy, that the first documented and scientific-founded distillation process was described. Wine itself was perceived to have medicinal properties, with alcohol as the 'active ingredient', and the extraction of the 'soul' or 'spirit' of the wine, through distillation, is what led to the naming of the distillates as 'spirits'. Until that time alcohol was a generic term applied to any product made by vaporising and condensation: the origins of the word come from the Arabic *al-kuhl*, and refers to this culture's practice of producing black powder by condensing the vapour of the metal antimony. The resulting black powder was used as eyeliner – still today called kohl! Only in the 16th century did 'alcohol' mean specifically those distilled 'sprits'.

While the medical fraternity were concerned with the surgical and health-giving properties of spirits, the alchemists were searching for a way of conferring everlasting life! The repeated distillation of spirits to a greater and greater purity led to the belief that the spirits could be the location of the Holy Grail. Arnaldo de Villanova, a Catalan physician in the 13th century coined the phrase *aqua vitae*, water of life, and the term lives on today in the Scandinavian aquavits and the French eau de vie. While the early distillates were of wine, it was not long before grain distillation began to produce the first whiskies and neutral spirits. Many of these contained herb and spice extracts, or were flavoured with fruits to enhance their medicinal properties, and to mask the raw taste and smell of the alcohol. Exactly where a distilled drink stops being a spirit and turns into a liqueur is problematic: to be a liqueur, a drink must have an aromatising element – or as in the case of Chartreuse, 130 of them!

Among these ancient liqueurs are kümmel, flavoured with caraway seeds; maraschino, infused with marasca cherries which once grew only on the Dalmatian coast of the former Yugoslavia; and ratafia (brandy mixed with fresh fruit juices), the most renowned being Pineau des Charentes. Chartreuse and Argentarium, are among the handful of liqueurs still produced by religious orders: Chartreuse, in both its yellow and green forms, is still made by the Carthusian monks at Voiron near Grenoble, as well as the original 'elixir', a premium version dating from 1605 and bottled at very high strength. A silent order, this no doubt helped to keep their recipe secret. Proceeds form the dale of Chartreuse are returned to the order's funds to pay for charitable works. Argentarium is made in a monastery in Lazio. northwest of Rome and is based on grape brandy flavoured with wild herbs picked from the hillsides by the monks. Argentarium is less well known than other 'monastic elixirs' largely because most of it is happily consumed locally! Benedictine was created in 1510 – or thereabouts – at the monastery at Fécamp in Normandy, northwest France, the exact formula of which is known only to three people at any one time. Production at the monastery ceased at the time of the French Revolution in 1789 when it was closed by Napoleon. Secular production began in the 1860s under Alexander Le Grand, following the discovery of the secret recipe in a pile of yellowing manuscripts.

The most elegant of all ingredients in a cocktail must surely be the king of wines: champagne. Said to have been 'stumbled upon' by a monk, Dom Petrus Perignon, in 1668 at the Abbey of Hautvilliers, this sparkling wine must not only have been grown in 'cork-popping' distance of Rheims and Epernay, but must also have been made by the champagne method: this means that the sparkle is made by a secondary fermentation in the bottle – not in a large vat, or by artificial carbonation. A vintage champagne may thus take eight years – or more – to reach perfection and maturity.

These wonderful ingredients have provided the bartender – and their customers – with the means to create drinks that first appeal to the eye, and then, with their subtle nuances of flavour, to the taste buds. The recipes that follow in this section include some of these rich and elegant ingredients: the recipes are easy to follow, but the drinks you will create can transform an occasion into a very special occasion.

Pineau-cchio

see page 105.

method:	MIXING GLASS
glass:	LIQUEUR OR CORDIAL GLASS

B & B Cocktail

One B is for Benedictine, the other for brandy – or preferably Cognac, which is deserving of such a fine companion.

Ingredients:

1 measure brandy or Cognac

1 measure Benedictine

Rich & Elegant

Method:

Place the ingredients in a mixing glass with some ice and stir. Strain into a cordial or liqueur glass.

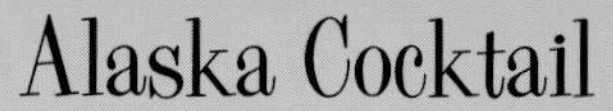

Alaska Cocktail

Rich & Elegant

Ingredients:
2 dashes orange bitters
1½ measures gin
¾ measure yellow Chartreuse

Method:
Stir together the ingredients in a mixing glass with some ice cubes. Strain into a cocktail glass.

method:	BUILD
glass:	WINE GLASS OR FLUTE

Alfonso

This champagne cocktail was created and named in honour of the Spanish King Alfonso XIII (1886–1941) who was deposed in 1931. Alfonso spent much of his exile in France, where he sampled this delight.

Rich & Elegant

Method:

Place the sugar cube into a chilled wine glass or flute, and soak it with the angostura bitters. Add a large ice cube and the Dubonnet. Finish with the champagne and stir. Squeeze a twist of lemon over the top and discard the peel.

Ingredients:

1 sugar lump
3 drops angostura bitters
1 measure Dubonnet
4 measures champagne

method:	MIXING GLASS
glass:	COCKTAIL

Alfonso Special

King Alfonso XIII of Spain appears to have drowned the sorrows of his exile quite well.

Ingredients:

1 measure Grand Marnier

¾ measure gin

¾ measure dry vermouth

4 dashes sweet vermouth

1 dash angostura bitters

Rich & Elegant

Method:

Place the ingredients in a mixing glass with some ice cubes and stir well. Strain into a cocktail glass.

method:	MIXING GLASS
glass:	COCKTAIL
garnish:	CHERRY AND SLICE OF LEMON

Bijou

The traditional recipe for this cocktail calls for Plymouth gin, a distinctly smooth gin made with the natural waters from Dartmoor, in the southwest of England.

Rich & Elegant

Method:

Place a few ice cubes in a mixing glass and pour in the ingredients. Stir and strain into a cocktail glass and garnish with the cherry and lemon slice.

Ingredients:

1 measure Plymouth gin
1 measure green Chartreuse
1 measure sweet red vermouth
1 dash orange bitters

method:	BUILD
glass:	GLASS OR FLUTE
garnish:	BLACK GRAPE

Black Tie

A chance to use Pineau des Charentes, a ratafia made in the Cognac region of France. Ratafia is not a geographical appellation, but derives from the ancient French practice of concluding a formal agreement, such as a legal transaction, with the Latin words 'rata fiat' *(let the deal be settled) and a shared drink – a 'ratifier'.*

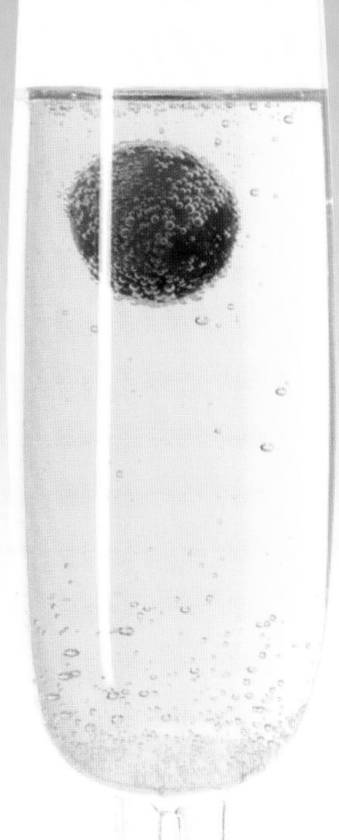

Rich & Elegant

Ingredients:

3 measures cold, white Pineau des Charentes
1½ measures champagne

Method:

Place the ingredients in a chilled wine glass or flute and garnish with a black grape. Watch the black grape go up and down!

method:	SHAKER
glass:	COCKTAIL
garnish:	LEMON TWIST

Green Lady

This recipe from Harry MacElhone's Harry's ABC of Mixing Cocktails *is credited to Georges Pesce of Fouquet's Bar in Paris. It's a delightfully elegant drink, and an opportunity to use both green and yellow Chartreuse along with gin.*

Ingredients:

2 measures gin
⅔ measure green Chartreuse
⅔ measure yellow Chartreuse

Rich & Elegant

Method:

Place the ingredients in a shaker with some ice cubes. Shake and strain into a cocktail glass and add the twist of lemon.

method:	BUILD
glass:	WINE GLASS
garnish:	SLICE OF ORANGE

Pineau-cchio

A lovely orange-wine flavour, and if you tell a little lie, your nose won't grow!

Ingredients:

1½ measures chilled, white Pineau des Charentes
½ measure cognac
½ measure triple sec/Cointreau

Method:

Moisten the rim of the wine glass with a little orange and dip into caster sugar. Fill the glass with broken ice and pour in the ingredients. Stir briefly and garnish with a slice of orange.

method: SHAKER

glass: COCKTAIL

Urbinos

A lovely raspberry-flavoured cocktail.

Rich & Elegant

Method:

Place all the ingredients in a shaker along with some ice cubes. Shake well and strain into a cocktail glass.

Ingredients:

3 measures chilled, white Pineau de Charentes
1 measure cognac
½ measure creme de framboise

B2 C2

This drink was invented in 1945 by none other than the United States 21st Army Corps. When they crossed the Rhine, they 'liberated' a Wehrmacht liquor store and what they found – the 2 Bs (brandy and Benedictine) and 2 Cs (Cointreau and champagne) – were immediately pressed into military service! You can also make this delicious formula in a jug and add chopped fruits in season to serve to your own platoon of guests.

Ingredients:

1 measure brandy
1 measure Benedictine
1 measure Cointreau
4 measures champagne

Rich & Elegant

Method:

Add the ingredients to a large wine glass!

method:	MIXING GLASS
glass:	COCKTAIL
garnish:	TWIST OF LEMON

Merry Widow Cocktail No. 1

One to hum along with to Franz Lehar's operetta of the same name!

Ingredients:

1¼ measures gin
1¼ measures dry vermouth
½ teaspoon Benedictine
½ teaspoon Pernod or Ricard
1 dash orange bitters

Rich & Elegant

Method:

Stir the ingredients in a mixing glass with some ice cubes. Strain into a cocktail glass and garnish with a twist of lemon.

Aqua Marina

Mint-flavoured champagne!

Ingredients:

4 measures champagne

1 measure vodka

½ measure green creme de menthe

½ measure lemon juice

Method:

Into a shaker with some ice cubes place the ingredients – except the champagne – and shake. Strain into a champagne flute and add the champagne.

method:	SHAKER
glass:	COLLINS
garnish:	SLICE OF LEMON AND A CHERRY

Shanghai Gin Fizz

A herb-flavoured delight that's as rich as silk!

Ingredients:

⅔ measure gin
⅔ measure Benedictine
⅔ measure yellow Chartreuse
⅔ measure lemon juice
½ measure sugar syrup
4 measures soda water

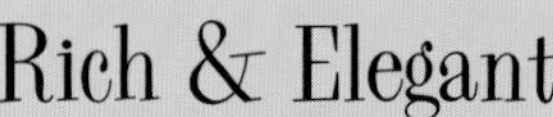

Rich & Elegant

Method:

Place all the ingredients – except the soda water – in a shaker with some ice cubes and shake well. Strain into a collins glass half-filled with ice and top with soda water. Garnish with a slice of lemon and a cherry, and serve with a muddler and straws.

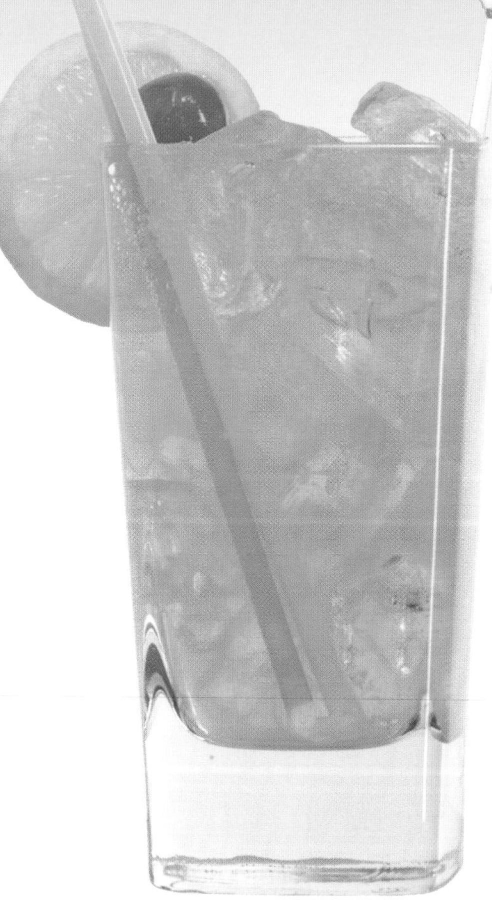

method: SHAKER

glass: HIGHBALL

Hong Kong Fizz

This magnificent concoction is credited to one Maude Jones, the Madame of a Hong Kong brothel in the 19th century. It is said that Ms. Jones consumed several of these drinks every day – before lunch!

Ingredients:

½ measure vodka
½ measure gin
½ measure Benedictine
½ measure yellow Chartreuse
½ measure green Chartreuse
½ measure lemon juice
4 measures soda water
½ teaspoon caster sugar

Rich & Elegant

Method:

Place some ice cubes into a shaker and pour in the ingredients – except the soda water. Shake vigourously so the caster sugar is dissolved. Strain into a highball glass half-filled with ice and top with soda water. Serve with straws and a muddler.

method: SHAKER

glass: COCKTAIL

Yellow Parrot

This luxurious cocktail was created around 1935 by Albert Coleman at the famous Stork Club in New York.

Ingredients:

1 measure Pernod or Ricard
1 measure yellow Chartreuse
1 measure apricot brandy

Rich & Elegant

Method:

Place the ingredients in a shaker with some ice cubes and shake well. Strain into a cocktail glass filled with crushed ice.

method:	SHAKER
glass:	OLD-FASHIONED

Worried Monk

Perhaps the Carthusian monks never envisaged their health-inducing elixir being mixed with other spirits for pure pleasure!

Ingredients:

- 1 measure white rum
- ½ measure coconut rum (Malibu or Batida de Coco)
- ¼ measure triple sec/Cointreau
- ¼ measure yellow Chartreuse
- ¾ measure lime juice
- ¼ measure orgeat (almond syrup)

Rich & Elegant

Method:

Place all the ingredients in a shaker with some ice cubes and shake well. Strain into an old-fashioned glass three-quarters filled with broken ice.

method: SHAKER
glass: COCKTAIL

Tovarich

A welcome opportunity to use kümmel, a caraway-flavoured liqueur, that was a favourite of Peter the Great of Russia. If you wanted an ultra-elegant version of this cocktail, try using goldwasser, flecked with real gold!

Ingredients:

1½ measures vodka
1 measure kümmel
juice of ½ lime

Rich & Elegant

Method:

Place some ice cubes into a shaker and squeeze in the juice of ½ lime. Pour in the kümmel and vodka and shake. Strain into a cocktail glass.

method:	SHAKER
glass:	COLLINS
garnish:	SEEDLESS GRAPES

Bacchanalian Cocktail

In honour of Bacchus, the Roman god of wine.

Ingredients:

1 measure white rum
½ measure brandy
½ measure yellow Chartreuse
2 measures red grape juice
1 measure orange juice
½ measure lime juice
3 measures lemonade

Rich & Elegant

Method:

Place all the ingredients except the lemonade in a shaker with some ice cubes. Shake well and strain into an ice-filled collins glass and garnish with the grapes.

method:	BUILD
glass:	CHAMPAGNE SAUCER
garnish:	2 CHERRIES ON A STICK

Marilyn Monroe

A classic champagne cocktail which uses Dom Perignon champagne – said to be the Hollywood legend's favourite.

Rich & Elegant

Method:

Add the ingredients to a well-chilled champagne saucer and garnish with the two cherries on a stick.

Ingredients:

1 measure Calvados
1 teaspoon grenadine
4 measures Dom Perignon

method:	MIXING GLASS
glass:	COCKTAIL
garnish:	TWIST OF LEMON

Rosalind Russell

Another great cocktail named after another of Hollywood's great ladies, this time from the 1930s. This subtle caraway-and-herb-flavoured cocktail uses aquavit, 'schnapps' from Denmark. Aquavit is a neutral grain and/or potato spirit, rectified to a very high degree of purity and then aromatised with fragrant spices. Try substituting aquavit for the vodka in a Bloody Mary!

Ingredients:

2 measures Danish aquavit
1 measure sweet red vermouth

Method:

Place the ingredients in a mixing glass with some ice cubes and stir. Strain into a chilled cocktail glass and add a twist of lemon.

method:	BUILD
glass:	COLLINS
garnish:	CHERRY AND SLICES OF ORANGE AND LEMON

B & B Collins

A wonderful hot-weather drink. The name Collins is thought to have come from one John Collins, a famous head waiter at Limmer's hotel and coffee house which was located in London's Conduit Street from 1790–1817.

Ingredients:

1½ measures brandy
½ measure Benedictine
1 measure lemon juice
1 measure sugar syrup
5 measures soda water

Rich & Elegant

Method:

Chill a collins glass and fill two thirds with ice. Pour in the lemon juice, sugar syrup and brandy and top with soda water. Sprinkle the Benedictine over the top and garnish with the cherry and slices of lemon and orange and serve with straws.

Chartreuse Cocktail

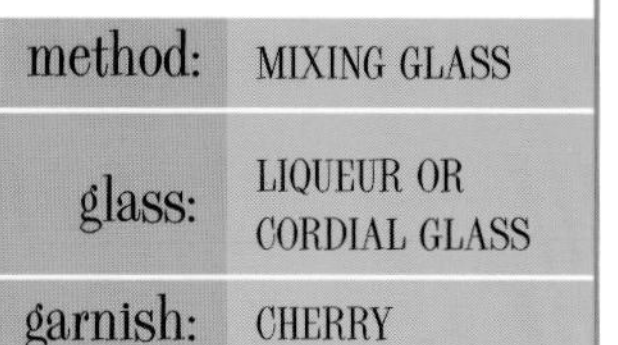

method:	MIXING GLASS
glass:	LIQUEUR OR CORDIAL GLASS
garnish:	CHERRY

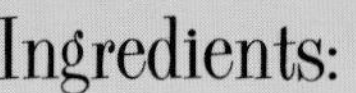

Ingredients:

1 measure yellow Chartreuse
1 measure cognac
½ measure dry vermouth

Rich & Elegant

Method:

Place ingredients in a mixing glass with some ice cubes and stir. Strain into a liqueur or cordial glass and garnish with a cherry.

method:	BUILD
glass:	COLLINS
garnish:	SPIRAL OF ORANGE

Chartreuse Cooler

This refreshingly fruity long drink is a wonderful way to indulge in Chartreuse.

Ingredients:

1 measure yellow Chartreuse
2 measures orange juice
½ measure lemon juice
3½ measures sparkling bitter lemon

Method:

Add some ice cubes to a collins glass, pour in the ingredients and top with the sparkling bitter lemon. Garnish with a spiral of orange.

method:	SHAKER
glass:	PILSNER
garnish:	CHERRY ON A STICK

Five Hundred Proof

A mixed drink for the connoisseur: the proof rating of the five spirits used in this drink should total over 500!

Ingredients:

- ½ measure over-proof white rum
- ½ measure 100-proof bourbon
- ½ measure green Chartreuse
- ½ measure 100-proof vodka
- ½ measure Southern Comfort
- 1 measure lemon juice
- 1 measure orange juice
- ½ measure sugar syrup
- ½ measure grenadine

Method:

Place all the ingredients in a shaker with some ice cubes and shake well. Strain into an ice-filled pilsner glass and garnish with a cherry on a stick.

method: MIXING GLASS

glass: LIQUEUR OR CORDIAL GLASS

Brandy Champarelle

The original recipe for this Champarelle – or Shamparelle – dates from the late 19th century when it was made as a pousse-café and used twice the volume of spirits and liqueurs as shown here!

Rich & Elegant

Method:

Place the ingredients in a mixing glass with some ice cubes and stir. Strain into a cordial or liqueur glass.

Ingredients:

¾ measure triple sec/Cointreau
¾ measure cognac
½ measure anis (substitute: Pernod or Ricard)
½ measure green Chartreuse

method:	MIXING GLASS
glass:	BRANDY SNIFTER

Brandy Fino

This very smooth drink is an opportunity to use one of Scotland's famous contributions to the world of liqueurs, glayva, created just after the Second World War, although the original formula for this whisky-based liqueur is much older and makes use of the finest Scottish heather, honey, herbs, and orange peel in its recipe.

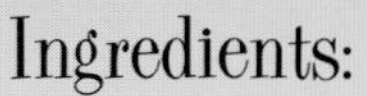

Ingredients:

1½ measures cognac

½ measure dry sherry

¼ measure glayva

Rich & Elegant

Method:

Place the ingredients in a mixing glass along with some ice cubes and stir. Strain into a brandy snifter.

method:	BUILD
glass:	OLD-FASHIONED
garnish:	TWIST OF LEMON

Bobby Burns

Staying 'north of the border', here's one drink that's perfect to celebrate Burn's Night for it is named after Scotland's most famous poet and song writer Robert Burns (1759–96), the composer of 'Auld Lang Syne'.

Variations:

Replace the Benedictine with a teaspoon of sugar syrup and a dash of angostura bitters to make a Flying Scotsman.

Replace the Benedictine with a teaspoon of sugar syrup alone and you have a Harry Lauder, another famous son of Scotland.

Ingredients:

1½ measures scotch
1½ measures sweet red (rosso) vermouth
1 teaspoon Benedictine

Rich & Elegant

Method:

To an old-fashioned glass, filled two-thirds with broken ice, add the liquid ingredients and the twist of lemon.

method:	BUILD
glass:	HIGHBALL
garnish:	LIME TWIST

Viking's Helmet

A gorgeous lime-flavoured long drink that uses aquavit and, if possible, Swedish vodka.

Ingredients:

1½ measures aquavit
¾ measure vodka – Swedish if possible!
¾ measure lime juice
⅓ measure pineapple syrup
3 measures ginger ale

Rich & Elegant

Method:

To a highball glass half-filled with ice cubes, add the ingredients and top with the ginger ale and add the twist of lime. *Skol!*

method:	SHAKER
glass:	COCKTAIL
garnish:	TWIST OF LEMON

K.G.B. Cocktail

Another chance to use the delicious caraway-flavoured kümmel.

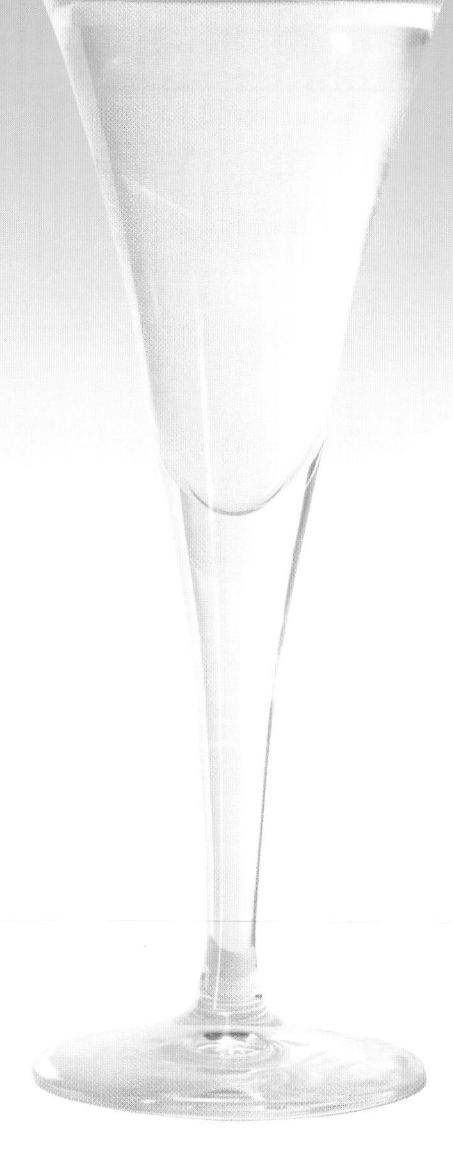

Ingredients:

½ measure kümmel
1½ measures gin
¼ teaspoon apricot brandy
¼ teaspoon lemon juice

Rich & Elegant

Method:

Place the ingredients in a cocktail shaker with some ice cubes and shake well. Strain into a well-chilled cocktail glass and add the twist of lemon.

method:	BUILD
glass:	COLLINS
garnish:	SLICE OF ORANGE AND A CHERRY

Lutter

Cognac is one of the finest spirits available to mankind and should be enjoyed at every opportunity! Purists might argue that such fine spirits should never be mixed, but the more adventurous maintain that clever combinations only enhance these already fine qualities. Try this delicious long drink and judge for yourself.

Rich & Elegant

Ingredients:

1 measure VSOP Cognac
½ measure vodka
½ measure Mandarine Napoleon
4 measures sparkling bitter lemon

Method:

Half fill a collins glass with broken ice and pour in the ingredients. Garnish with the orange slice and the cherry and serve with straws.

method:	BUILD
glass:	FLUTE
garnish:	SMALL ROSE PETAL

This delicious and very beautiful champagne cocktail is perfect for a celebration – an engagement, a wedding, an anniversary, a birthday – or just for dinner à deux *perhaps!*

Rich & Elegant

Method:

Simply add the ingredients to a chilled champagne flute and float a small rose petal on top.

Ingredients:

1 teaspoon filtered lemon juice
1 teaspoon blue Curaçao
1 teaspoon amaretto
3½ measures champagne

method:	BUILD
glass:	CHAMPAGNE SAUCER

Hemingway

As well as being a daiquiri fan, the great American novelist, Ernest Hemingway, created this champagne and Pernod drink. When he gave the recipe to Esquire *magazine, Hemingway called his drink Death in the Afternoon and suggested that three – or five – of these sipped slowly would do the trick!*

Rich & Elegant

Method:

Pour the Pernod into the champagne saucer and add the chilled champagne until the whole mix becomes opalescent.

Ingredients:

1½ measures Pernod
chilled champagne

method:	BUILD
glass:	WINE GLASS
garnish:	SLICE OF ORANGE AND A CHERRY

Pernod Fizz

Another glorious mix of Pernod and champagne, but this time with a little mandarin juice.

Ingredients:

¾ measure Pernod
1 measure mandarin juice
chilled champagne

Rich & Elegant

Method:

Fill a good sized wine glass ¾ full with broken ice. Pour in the Pernod and mandarin juice and top with chilled champagne. Garnish with the slice of orange and the cherry.

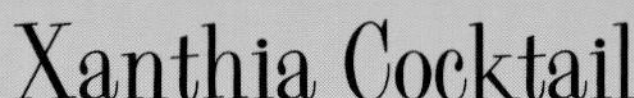

Xanthia Cocktail

Ingredients:

I measure gin

I measure yellow Chartreuse

I measure cherry brandy

Rich & Elegant

Method:

Place all the ingredients in a mixing glass with some ice cubes and stir. Strain into a cocktail glass.

method:	BUILD
glass:	FLUTE
garnish:	TWIST OF ORANGE

Tomorrow We Sail

A name that conjures up the luxurious ocean liners, but one to enjoy at any port of call!

Ingredients:

1 teaspoon triple sec/Cointreau
½ measure dark rum
½ measure LBV port
chilled champagne

Rich & Elegant

Method:

Pour the triple sec/Cointreau, rum and port into the Champagne flute and add the chilled champagne and garnish with a twist of orange.

Mule's Hind Leg

A fruity-herb flavour that packs a kick too!, this drink blends 'old world' gin and Benedictine with 'new world' maple syrup and applejack.

Ingredients:

½ measure gin

½ measure applejack (substitute: Calvados, apple brandy)

⅓ measure Benedictine

⅓ measure apricot brandy

⅓ measure maple syrup

Rich & Elegant

Method:

Place all the ingredients in a shaker with some ice cubes and shake. Strain into an old-fashioned glass three-quarter filled with broken ice.

method: SHAKER
glass: COCKTAIL

Spring Feeling Cocktail

As soon as the first spring flowers appear, it's a good time to indulge in one of these and feel your sap start to rise!

Rich & Elegant

Method:

Shake the ingredients with some ice cubes and strain into a cocktail glass.

Ingredients:

1½ measures gin
¾ measure green Chartreuse
1 tablespoon of lemon juice

St. Patrick's Day

A very pleasant change from stout on March 17th.

Ingredients:

1 measure green creme de menthe
1 measure green Chartreuse
1 measure Irish whiskey – of course!
1 dash angostura bitters

Rich & Elegant

Method:

Place the ingredients in a mixing glass with some ice cubes and stir. Strain into a cocktail glass and say Slainte!

method:	BUILD
glass:	FLUTE
garnish:	HALF A SLICE OF ORANGE AND CHERRY

Horn of Plenty

In classical mythology, the Horn of Plenty, or cornucopia, is said to have been the horn of the goat belonging to the nymph, Amalthaea, who lost it when she fought in the form of a bull with Hercules. By magic, the horn then contained an abundant and endless supply of of food and drink, while Amalthaea was transformed into the star Capella.

Rich & Elegant

Method:

Add the first three ingredients to a chilled champagne glass and top with the champagne. Garnish with the half slice of orange and a cherry.

Ingredients:

1/3 measure Grand Marnier
1/3 measure Campari
1/4 measure grenadine
chilled champagne

method:	BUILD
glass:	CHAMPAGNE SAUCER OR FLUTE

Whoopee Cocktail

'Don't forget folks, that's what you get, folks, for making whoopee'. This champagne delight comes from Harry MacElhone's Harry's ABC of Mixing Cocktails.

Ingredients:

1 lump of ice
½ measure Curaçao
½ measure Cognac
chilled champagne

Rich & Elegant

Method:

Place the ice cube into the champagne saucer or flute. Pour in the Curaçao and Cognac and fill the glass with chilled champagne.

Fruity Beauties

If you like your cocktails and mixed drinks to taste fruity, then you're in for a treat. There are hundreds of exciting and delicious recipes from which to choose: from sharp and tangy, to smooth and sweet, and there are short and tall drinks to select from. 'Fruity' cocktails and mixed drinks may be fruit flavoured because they have been prepared with fresh fruit juices. There are so many tropical and exotic fruits readily available in supermarkets for you to juice yourself, or as ready-prepared juices, either frozen or in cartons. Another way of creating fruity flavours is with the use of liqueurs and liqueur brandies and there are some exciting flavours available from orange and mandarin to melon and pear.

A liqueur is any spirit-based drink to which flavouring elements have been added. This is usually done by infusion and, in most cases, the flavours are further enhanced by sweeteners. Sometimes the flavourings are simply soaked or macerated in an alcoholic base, other times the flavourings themselves are subjected to the distillation process.

Many liqueurs are ancient in origin and were developed from the practice of adding wonderfully aromatic ingredients – such as herbs, flowers, nuts, seeds, spices and plant roots – to the earliest distilled spirits in order to cover up the unappealing taste or rawness of the spirit. In some

Liberator

see page 166.

cases these liqueurs were invested with health-giving properties and were regarded as 'tonics'. The monastic orders, such as the Benedictine and Carthusian, had an unsurpassed knowledge of herbs and their preservative and medicinal qualities. For centuries, in addition to acting as the local 'hospitals' and dispensing advise and herbs from their monastery gardens, the monks also began to formulate their liqueurs.

In later centuries, liqueurs became widely regarded as after-dinner digestifs and were favoured by those who preferred a less 'strong' alternative to traditional drinks such as Cognac. This practice led liqueurs to become regarded as 'ladylike' drinks, which was further compounded by serving them in tiny, delicate glasses. Fortunately, the cocktail era of the 1920s and 1930s freed these lovely liqueurs from both their medicinal (although many still believe in their prophylactic properties) and over-refined, ladylike cultures and soon they were transforming the old mixed drinks like punches, smashes, fizzes and cups, into daring and dazzling drinks.

Marimba
see page 169.

Some of the most popular liqueurs include Curaçao, a brandy-based sprit flavoured with the peel of bitter oranges. There are many brands available, but the most well-known brand of colourless Curaçao is Cointreau. Other Curaçao are available in a range of colours – bright blue, dark green, red and yellow used both for adding flavour and colour – but the flavour is always orange. Other orange-flavoured liqueurs are mersin, a Turkish version of Curaçao, Van der Hum (which literally translates as 'what's his name'), Grand Marnier made from the juice of Caribbean oranges and top-quality Cognac, and Mandarine Napoleon, a favourite tipple of Napoleon I, made with the skins of Sicilian mandarins. Maraschino is another ancient liqueur. This clear, colourless liqueur is derived from an infusion of pressed cherry skins in a cherrystone distillate. A more recent 'invention' from the 1980s is Midori, a bright green

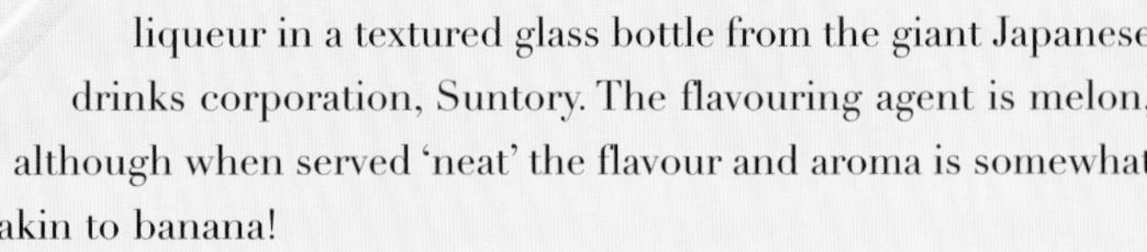

Titanic Uplift

see page 163.

liqueur in a textured glass bottle from the giant Japanese drinks corporation, Suntory. The flavouring agent is melon, although when served 'neat' the flavour and aroma is somewhat akin to banana!

A large range of liqueurs use the prefix 'crème de' in their names. Originally, the term 'crème' was used to indicate that these were sweetened liqueurs, distinct from dry spirits like Cognac. Most of the crème liqueurs originated in France – the Marie Brizard company founded in the 18th century is still the leading producer – but other companies, notably Bols and De Kuypers of Holland also produce a range. The variety of flavours is enormous, but most commonly seen are crème de banane (banana), cassis (blackcurrant), framboise (raspberry), fraise (strawberry). More obscure, but no less exciting, are crème de mûre (blackberry), myrtille (bilberry) and pêche (peach). In addition to fruit, crème liqueurs are also flavoured with mint, (crème de menthe, in both white and green versions), almonds (noyau), vanilla, chocolate, coffee, tea and violets!

Liqueur brandies, strictly speaking, belong to the same category as liqueurs with the prefix 'crème de', since they are not brandies in the true sense, but sweetened, coloured drinks based on grape brandy to which fruit flavours have been added. There are essentially three fruit brandies: cherry, apricot and peach.

America's foremost liqueur is undoubtedly Southern Comfort, the exact formula of which – like so many liqueurs – is a closely guarded secret. What we do know is that the finest American whiskey is used to blend with a peach flavour. Whiskey and peach juice had for many years been a favourite combination in the bars of the southern states of America.

Arrowhead

A delightful fruit-rum flavour, hints of peach, bananas and citrus fruits. Traditionally served on the rocks, it's also very nice long, with more lemonade!

Ingredients:

1 measure dark rum
½ measure Southern Comfort
½ measure creme de banane
¼ measure lime juice
2½ measures (or more) lemonade

Method:

Add the ingredients to an old-fashioned glass, three-quarters full of broken ice. If you prefer a longer drink, use a collins glass, and top with more lemonade.

method:	BUILD
glass:	HIGHBALL
garnish:	FRUIT IN SEASON

Beef Salad

The 'beef' comes from Beefeater gin, the 'salad' from its delightful green colour courtesy of the Midori and the green Chartreuse.

Ingredients:

1½ measures Beefeater gin

½ measure Midori melon liqueur

1 teaspoon green Chartreuse

4½ measures sparkling bitter lemon

Fruity Beauties

Method:

Add the liquid ingredients to an ice-filled highball glass and garnish with fruits in season. Serve with straws.

How about a Beef Salad on Rye? Just add ½ measure rye whiskey!

method:	BUILD
glass:	HIGHBALL
garnish:	CHERRY AND SLICE OF LEMON

Blue Lagoon

Blue Curaçao hit the bar scene in 1960 and this fabulous orange-lemon flavoured drink was created at Harry's Bar in Paris by Andy MacElhone, the famous son of the famous Harry MacElhone. Originally, Andy served this drink short, with one measure of lemon juice in place of the lemonade. Both ways are equally fine.

Ingredients:

1 measure vodka

1 measure blue Curaçao

4 measures lemonade

Method:

Add the ingredients to highball glass filled with ice and garnish with cherry and slice of lemon.

method:	SHAKER
glass:	HIGHBALL
garnish:	CHERRY AND A CUBE OF PINEAPPLE ON A STICK

Buttock Clencher

The 'fun and funky' name betrays the modern origins of this drink – as does the inclusion of tequila which, although it has been made for centuries in its native Mexico, is a relative newcomer to the cocktail scene. Try this pineapple-flavoured delight.

Ingredients:

1 measure silver tequila
1 measure gin
¼ measure Midori melon liqueur
2 measures pineapple juice
2 measures lemonade

Method:

Place all the ingredients, except the lemonade, in a shaker with two to three ice cubes. Shake and strain into an ice-filled highball glass and add the lemonade. Garnish with the cherry and pineapple cube.

method: SHAKER

glass: OLD-FASHIONED

Cactus Juice

Here's another way to enjoy the juice of the Agave tequiliana *and an opportunity to use Scotland's fine contribution to the world's classic liqueurs, Drambuie. A unique blend of whisky (of course), heather (naturally), honey and herbs based on a recipe said to have been given as a reward to Captain Mackinon in 1745 following the defeat of Bonnie Prince Charlie at the Battle of Culloden. Mackinon was the protector of the 'Pretender' after the prince was ferried 'over the sea to Skye' and on to safety in France. While the story may be a little invented, the Mackinon family are still making Drambuie in Edinburgh, Scotland.*

Ingredients:

2 measures gold tequila

1 teaspoon Drambuie

1 measure lemon juice

1 teaspoon caster sugar

Method:

Dissolve the sugar in the lemon juice and pour into a shaker with a glass full of broken ice cubes. Add the tequila and Drambuie and shake well. Pour, unstrained, into an old-fashioned glass.

method:	SHAKE
glass:	GOBLET OR OVERSIZED WINE GLASS
garnish:	FRUIT IN SEASON

Chaos Calmer

Orange-flavoured gin makes a very pleasant change from the usual gin-tonic combination.

Ingredients:

1½ measures gin
¼ measure triple sec/Cointreau
1½ measures orange juice
¾ measure lime juice
1 teaspoon grenadine

Method:

Place all the ingredients into a shaker with a glassful of broken ice and shake well. Pour, unstrained, into a goblet or oversized wine glass and garnish with fruit in season.

method:	SHAKER
glass:	CHAMPAGNE SAUCER OR COCKTAIL GLASS
garnish:	SLICE OF ORANGE SPEARED WITH A CHERRY

Cherry Blossom

Cherry brandy may be one of the very few liqueurs to have been 'invented' in England. Said to be the creation of one Thomas Grant from Kent, the 'garden of England', who made his version with black morello cherries. While fruity, it's got a kick to it: cherry brandy was the ruin of the dissolute Prince Regent, later King George IV.

Ingredients:

1½ measures cherry brandy
1 measure brandy
¼ measure triple sec/Cointreau
¼ measure lemon juice
⅓ measure egg white
1 teaspoon grenadine
¼ measure sugar syrup

Method:

Rim the champagne saucer or cocktail glass with a little grenadine and dip into some caster sugar. Place the ingredients in a shaker with two or three ice cubes and shake well. Strain into the 'frosted' champagne saucer and garnish with the slice of orange and the cherry.

method: BUILD

glass: HIGHBALL

Codswallop

Believe it or not, in the 1850s Mr. Hiram Codd patented a soda water-lemonade bottle which was sealed with a glass marble in the neck. The marble was held in place by the pressure of the fizzy drink, and to release the contents you had to 'wallop' (hit) the top of the bottle to break the seal.

Method:

Add all the ingredients to an ice-filled highball glass and top with cold lemonade.

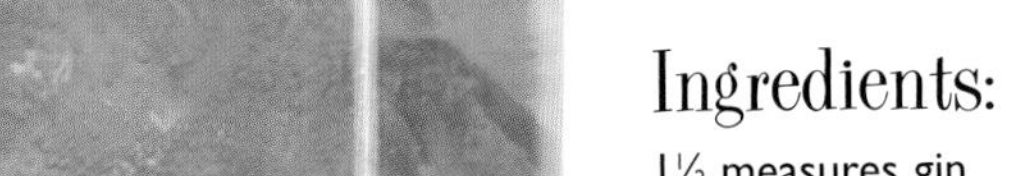

Ingredients:

1½ measures gin
⅓ measure Campari
⅓ measure creme de framboise
⅓ measure lime juice
4 measures lemonade

method:	BUILD
glass:	HIGHBALL
garnish:	MINT SPRIG (OPTIONAL)

Escape Route

This refreshing strawberry-flavoured drink traditionally used Punt e Mes, one of the world's most popular vermouths. In 1786 Antonio Carpano opened the Carpano Bar behind the Turin Stock Exchange, Italy, where he offered variations of the basic Carpano vermouth – some sweet, some bitter. Stockbrokers who regularly frequented the bar began to grade the relative bitterness of the vermouths in 'points'. In 1876, Punt e Mes (point and a half) was launched commercially.

Ingredients:

1 measure golden rum

1 measure Punt e Mes

½ measure creme de fraise

4 measures lemonade

Method:

Simply add the ingredients to an ice-filled highball glass and garnish with a sprig of mint and escape into pure bliss.

method:	STIR
glass:	BRANDY SNIFTER

Connoisseur's Treat

An orange-brandy flavour with just a hint of anise (liquorice), almonds and vanilla, courtesy of the golden-yellow Italian liqueur, Galliano.

Ingredients:

1½ measures Cognac

½ measure Galliano

½ Grand Marnier

Method:

Stir and strain the ingredients into a brandy snifter.

method:	SHAKER
glass:	HIGHBALL

Even Pair

The flavour of this gin-based mixed drink comes from pear liqueur. There are a number on the market including Poire William from France, named after the variety of pear used in its production, Italy's Pera Segnana, and variations from Germany and Switzerland. Never failing to raise an eyebrow and debate as to 'how do they do that' is the 'novelty' Poire Prisonniere (literally, imprisoned pear) where the pears are painstakingly grown in bottles while they are still attached to a tree: each fruit effectively has its own individual green house!

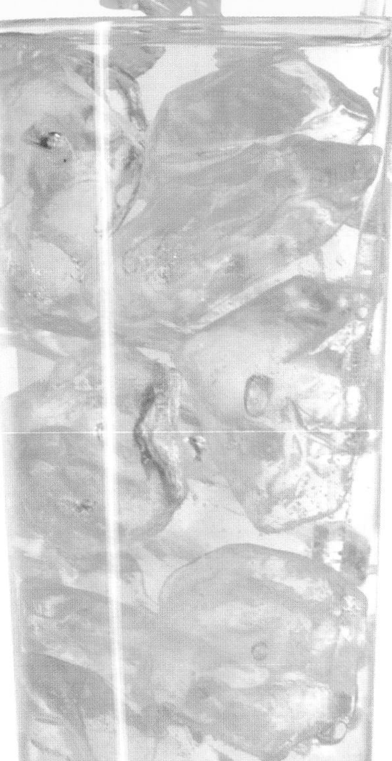

Ingredients:

1 measure gin
1 measure dry vermouth
⅓ measure pear liqueur
4 measures tonic water

Method:

Place all the ingredients except the tonic water into a shaker with two or three ice cubes. Shake well and strain into an ice-filled highball glass. Top with tonic.

method:	BUILD
glass:	PINA COLADA GLASS, OR OVERSIZED WINE GLASS
garnish:	SPRIG OF MINT

Fly Swatter

The original recipe calls for raki, the aniseed-tinged drink of Greece and Turkey. You can use Pernod or Ricard, the most familiar pastis on the market today.

Fruity Beauties

Method:

Add the ingredients to a piña colada or oversized wine glass filled with broken ice. Add a sprig of mint and serve with straws.

Ingredients:

- 1 measure Cognac
- 1 measure whisky
- 1 teaspoon Pernod or Ricar
- 3 measures mandarin juice
- 2 measures pineapple juice

method:	SHAKER
glass:	PINA COLADA, OR OVERSIZED WINE GLASS
garnish:	SLICE OF PINEAPPLE AND A CHERRY

Hurricane

One to enjoy when you've got to ride out a storm!

Ingredients:

1½ measures dark rum
1 measure light rum
1 measure lime juice
2 measures passion fruit juice
1 measure pineapple juice
1 measure orange juice
½ measure blackcurrant syrup

Method:

Place the ingredients in a shaker with two or three ice cubes and shake well. Strain into an ice-filled piña colada or oversized wine glass, filled with broken ice. Garnish with the slice of pineapple and the cherry and serve with straws.

method: SHAKER
glass: OLD-FASHIONED

Duck Soup

Homage to the Marx brothers perhaps? Break out that apricot brandy for a real treat.

Ingredients:

2 measures bourbon
½ measure apricot brandy
¾ measure lemon juice
¾ measure pineapple juice
½ teaspoon caster sugar

Method:

Dissolve the sugar in the lemon juice and add, along with other ingredients, to a shaker with two or three ice cubes. Shake well and strain into old fashioned glass three-quarters filled with broken ice.

method:	SHAKER
glass:	COCKTAIL
garnish:	CHERRY, GREEN PREFERABLY!

Evergreen

One to make you burst into song!

Ingredients:

1 measure creme de banane
½ measure Midori melon liqueur
½ measure blue Curaçao
½ measure gin
2 measures white grape juice

Method:

Shake all the ingredients in a shaker with two or three ice cubes and strain into a chilled cocktail glass. Garnish with a green cherry.

method:	SHAKER
glass:	OLD-FASHIONED
garnish:	SLICE OF ORANGE AND A CHERRY

Kiss and Tell

One to console yourself with while you discuss matters with tabloid journalists!

Ingredients:

1 measure vodka

½ measure Galliano

¼ measure dry vermouth

1 teaspoon blue Curaçao

2 measures orange juice

1 measure passion fruit juice

Method:

Place the ingredients in a shaker with a glass full of broken ice and shake well. Pour, unstrained, into an old-fashioned glass. Garnish with the slice of orange and the cherry.

method: BUILD

glass: OLD-FASHIONED

Firebird

In the ballet of the same name, a high golden fence protects the garden of golden fruits grown of the sinister Katschei, who has imprisoned the lovely princess. The firebird tries to steal the golden fruit but is captured by Prince Ivan, who lets her go in exchange for one of her magical feathers: armed with this, Ivan is assured of the firebird's help should he need it. Prince Ivan then discovers the beautiful captive princess who warns him that Katschei will turn him to stone if discovered. When this happens, Ivan waves the firebird's feather in Katschei's face and the firebird appears, forcing the evil monsters who attend the magician to dance until they collapse. The firebird shows Ivan a great golden egg, which holds the soul of the magician. Ivan throws the egg into the air, and when it falls, it breaks and Katschei dies. Ivan marries his princess and the firebird flies away forever. This has absolutely nothing to do with the cocktail, but it's a great ballet, choreographed by George Balanchine to magnificent score by Igor Stravinsky!

Fruity Beauties

Ingredients:

1½ measures silver tequila
½ measure creme de banane
½ measure lime juice
2 measures lemonade

Method:

Add the ingredients to an old fashioned glass three-quarters filled with broken ice. Dream of a handsome prince/beautiful princess/big bird.

method:	BUILD
glass:	OLD-FASHIONED
garnish:	FRUIT IN SEASON, TWIST OF LEMON

Santa Cruz Fix

The original recipe for this cherry-rum drink calls for Santa Cruz rum, but you can use a good, dark rum if you wish.

Method:

Add to old-fashioned glass filled with crushed ice and garnish with fruit in season and a twist of lemon. Serve with straws.

Ingredients:

2 measures dark rum
1 measure cherry brandy
1 measure lemon juice
¾ measure sugar syrup

method:	SHAKER
glass:	HIGHBALL
garnish:	SLICE OF ORANGE AND PINEAPPLE

Lady Killer

Delightful passion fruit flavour.

Ingredients:

1 measure gin
¾ measure apricot brandy
¾ measure Cointreau
2 measures passion fruit juice
2 measures pineapple juice

Method:

Place the ingredients in a shaker with two or three ice cubes and shake well. Strain into a highball glass filled with ice and garnish with the orange and pineapple slices.

method: BUILD

glass: PILSNER

Paris Opera

Try this combination of aniseed and orange flavours.

Ingredients:

1 measure Mandarine Napoleon
1 measure Pernod
5 measures lemonade

Method:

Add the ingredients to a pilsner glass filled with broken ice.

method:	SHAKER
glass:	HIGHBALL

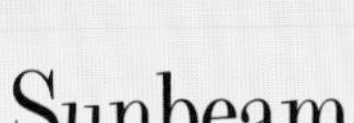

Sunbeam

A play on the producers names: Midori melon liqueur by Suntory and bourbon by Jim Beam.

Ingredients:

1 measure Midori melon liqueur
1 measure Jim Beam bourbon
½ measure creme de banane
2 measure mandarin juice
2 measures pineapple juice
¼ measure grenadine

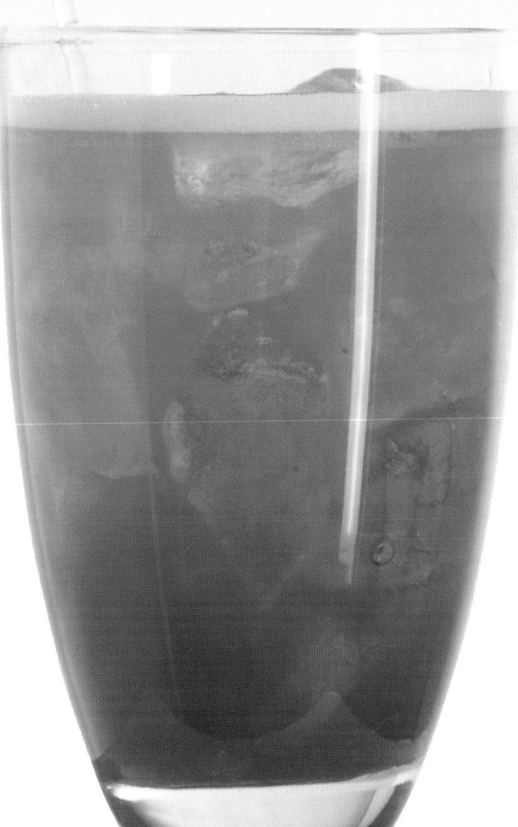

Method:

Place all the ingredients except the grenadine into a shaker with two or three ice cubes and shake well. Strain into an ice-filled highball glass, then add the grenadine – but do not stir.

method:	SHAKE
glass:	PINA COLADA OR OVERSIZED WINE GLASS
garnish:	SPENT SHELL OF LIME

Sun City

A great fruity flavour that's perfect for a hot sunny afternoon.

Ingredients:

1 measure light rum
½ measure dark rum
½ measure Galliano
½ measure apricot brandy
2 measures pineapple juice
juice of ¼ lime
4 measures lemonade

Method:

Place all the ingredients except the lemonade into a shaker with two or three ice cubes. Shake well and strain into ice filled piña colada or oversized wine glass. Drop in the spent shell of the lime and top up with lemonade. Serve with straws.

method:	SHAKER
glass:	COLLINS
garnish:	3 MELON BALLS COLOURED GREEN, RED AND ORANGE

Titanic Uplift

It was said of the enormously expensive, but disastrous box office flop, Raise the Titanic, *that it would have been cheaper to drain the Atlantic. Here's how to do it yourself!*

Ingredients:

2 measures Midori melon liqueur
1 measure gin
4 measures orange juice

Method:

Place the ingredients in a shaker with some ice cubes and shake vigourously. Strain into a collins glass three-quarters filled with broken ice. Garnish with the three coloured melon balls. Serve with a straw.

method:	SHAKER
glass:	COCKTAIL
garnish:	SLICE OF LIME AND A CHERRY

Hen Night Zipper-ripper

What more can we say?

Method:

Place all the ingredients in a shaker with some ice cubes and shake vigourously. Strain into a cocktail glass and garnish with the slice of lime and the cherry.

Ingredients:

1½ measures white rum
1 measure advocaat
¾ measure mandarin juice
¾ measure lime juice
¼ measure grenadine

method:	SHAKER
glass:	COLLINS
garnish:	SPRIG OF MINT AND A CHERRY

Trouser Rouser

If the Hen Night Zipper-ripper is for the girls, then this must be for the 'stags'!

Ingredients:

1½ measures scotch

½ measure creme de banane

2 measures mango juice

1 measure pineapple juice

½ measure lime juice

1 teaspoon egg white

Method:

Place all the ingredients in a shaker with some ice cubes and shake well. Strain into a Collins glass three-quarters filled with broken ice and garnish with the mint sprig and cherry.

method:	SHAKER
glass:	COCKTAIL
garnish:	SLICE OF LIME

Liberator

Feel free with this mango-flavoured cocktail.

Method:

Place all the ingredients in a shaker with ice cubes and shake well. Strain into a cocktail glass and garnish with a slice of lime.

Ingredients:

1½ measures vodka

½ measure Midori melon liqueur

2 measures mango juice

½ measure lime juice

Pan-galactic Gargle Blaster

You've heard of it, so now's your chance to try it!

Ingredients:

1½ measures Midori melon liqueur
½ measure white rum (over-proof rum if available)
½ measure lime juice
¼ measure pineapple syrup
1½ measures lemonade

Method:

Place all the ingredients except the lemonade in a shaker with some ice cubes and shake well. Strain into a flute and add the lemonade.

(with grateful acknowledgement to the late, great Douglas Adams!)

method:	SHAKER
glass:	COLLINS
garnish:	SLICE OF LIME AND A CHERRY

Zulu

Raise your glass and give the traditional Zulu toast of 'Ooogy Wawa'.

Ingredients:

1 measure dark rum
1 measure dark creme de cacao
½ measure creme de banane
1 measure lime juice
1 teaspoon grenadine
1 teaspoon Pernod or Ricard
4 measures cold cola

Method:

Place all the ingredients except the cola in a shaker with ice cubes and shake well. Strain into an ice-filled collins glass and add the cola. Garnish with the lime slice and cherry.

method:	SHAKER
glass:	COCKTAIL
garnish:	ORANGE AND PINEAPPLE SLICES

Marimba

Like the musical instrument, this tropical-fruit-flavoured cocktail is certain to get you dancing.

Ingredients:

1 measure Southern Comfort
½ measure gin
¼ measure amaretto
1 measure pineapple juice
1 measure mango juice
¼ measure lime juice

Method:

Place all the ingredients in a shaker with some ice cubes and shake rhythmically. Strain into a cocktail glass and garnish with pineapple and orange slices.

method: SHAKER

glass: HIGHBALL

Woo Woo

Once this was a Teeny-Weeny Woo-Woo and was famous for about 15 minutes in the 1980s when peach schnapps became the flavour 'du jour'. *It's a shame it went out of fashion because it really is a lovely cranberry-peach flavour.*

Ingredients:

1½ measures peach schnapps

1 measure vodka

4 measures cranberry juice

Method:

Place the ingredients in a shaker with some ice cubes and shake well. Strain into an ice-filled highball glass.

method:	BUILD
glass:	HIGHBALL
garnish:	CHERRY AND LEMON SLICE

Arctic Summer

A delicious blend of apricot and lemon.

Ingredients:

1½ measures gin

¾ measure apricot brandy

1 teaspoon grenadine

4 measures sparkling bitter lemon

Method:

Add to an ice-filled highball glass and garnish with a cherry and slice of lemon.

Smooth & Creamy

Brandy Alexander
see page 179.

In addition to spirits, liqueurs and juices, a whole variety of mixed drinks in the cocktail barman's repertoire include those made with the addition of milk, cream, coconut cream or egg whites and egg yolks. The range of drinks in this category include both 'short' cocktails and 'long' mixed drinks such as the traditional classics – the wonderfully named Flips, Milk Punches, Cows and Puffs – as well as the 'old favourites', the Brandy Alexander (and its relatives) and Egg Nogg. In addition, modern bartenders have developed a whole range of exciting drinks to tantalise the taste buds of new consumers. These include the famously named Love in the Afternoon and the Fluffy Duck. The use of eggs, cream and milk is to produce a drink that is pleasing to the eye because of its creamy or foamy texture. Coconut cream does the same but also gives drinks a slightly sweet, coconut flavour. All these ingredients 'smooth' out and 'cover up' the sharpness of the drink's spirit or liqueur base. Using these ingredients also lengthens the 'reaction time': eggs, cream and milk and coconut cream will not

Caribbean Sunset
see page 188.

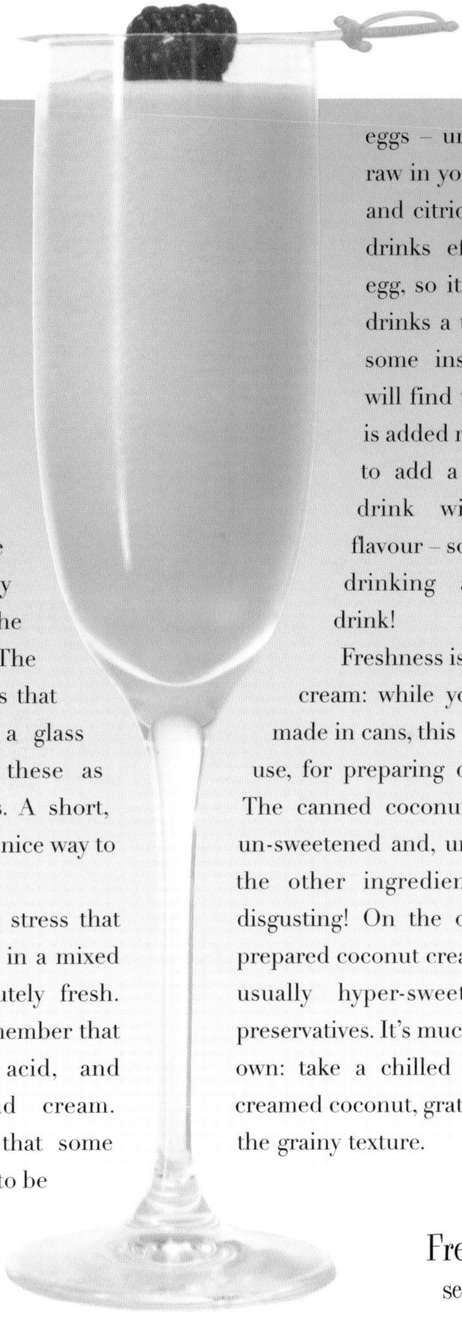

make a drink 'milder' – they will only make a drink taste less strong and postpone the effects of the alcohol in your system. Sooner or later, the alcohol will reach the bloodstream! Don't be fooled, creamy drinks can be lethal! They taste so nice and 'harmless' that the temptation is to have another, so beware, because you'll soon feel the cumulative effects! Creamy drinks also don't stimulate the appetite – they smother it. The richness of these drinks means that they are almost a meal in a glass themselves, so don't serve these as aperitifs or pre-dinner drinks. A short, creamy drink is however a very nice way to end a delicious dinner!

It shouldn't be necessary to stress that if you use eggs, cream or milk in a mixed drink, they should be absolutely fresh. It's also important that you remember that citrus juices are full of acid, and this will curdle milk and cream. Consequently, you will find that some recipes call for the ingredients to be blended first and the cream or milk added last. The exact opposite is true for eggs – unless you fancy them raw in your drink! The alcohol and citric acid content of the drinks effectively 'cooks' the egg, so it is best to give these drinks a thorough 'mixing'. In some instances, though, you will find that a little egg white is added right at the end: this is to add a 'silver froth' to the drink without adding any flavour – so don't think you'll be drinking an eggy flavoured drink!

Freshness is also true for coconut cream: while you can buy it ready-made in cans, this is usually for culinary use, for preparing dishes such as curry. The canned coconut cream is generally un-sweetened and, until it is cooked with the other ingredients, it tastes pretty disgusting! On the other hand, specially prepared coconut cream made for drinks is usually hyper-sweet and is full of preservatives. It's much better to make your own: take a chilled hard block of pure creamed coconut, grate it up to break down the grainy texture.

French Kiss
see page 190.

method:	BUILD
glass:	COLLINS
garnish:	SPRINKLE OF NUTMEG

Brown Cow

Cows are long drinks made with milk – a bit like a milkshake – but with a kick! Brandy and rum are among the most popular spirits used, but this Brown Cow is coffee flavoured: you can use Tia Maria or kahlua.

1½ measured Tia Maria or kahlu
6 measures cold milk

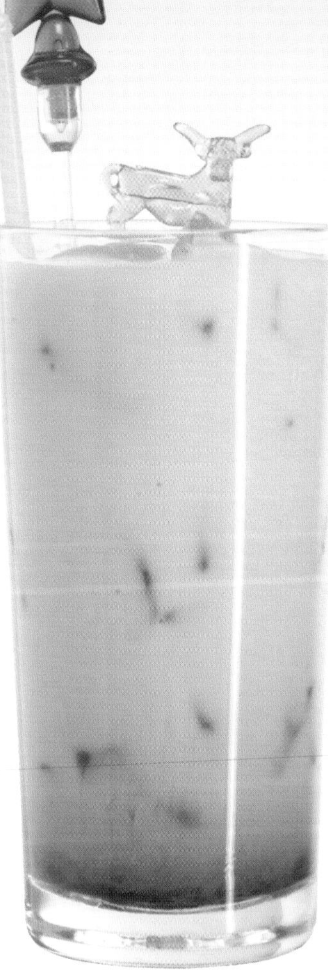

Smooth & Creamy

Method:

Fill a collins glass with ice cubes and pour in the coffee liqueur and milk. Sprinkle grated nutmeg on top. Serve with a stirrer and a straw.

method:	SHAKER
glass:	COLLINS OR HIGHBALL
garnish:	CHERRY ON A STICK, SPRINKLE OF NUTMEFG OR CINNAMON

Comfortable Milk Punch

Milk punches are a little similar to cows, but with the addition of a little sugar syrup to sweeten them up. Punches are also shaken and poured over rocks in a tall glass. A single spirit, such as brandy, rum, rye, bourbon or Scotch can be used. This recipe adds a touch of peach by using Southern Comfort.

Ingredients:

2 measures Southern Comfort

½ measure sugar syrup

5 measures cold, full-cream milk

Method:

Fill a collins or highball glass with ice cubes. Add a few ice cubes to a shaker and pour in the ingredients and shake well. Strain and pour into glass filled with ice cubes. Garnish with a cherry on a stick and a sprinkling of nutmeg or cinnamon. Serve with a straw.

method: SHAKER

glass: GOBLET OR BRANDY SNIFTER

Brandy Puff

Before Prohibition, puffs were enormously popular drinks in the United States. Any spirit can be used: whisky and rum go well with milk, and so does brandy. If you're feeling adventurous, try a Gin Puff.

Ingredients:

2 measures brandy

3 measures cold milk

3 measures soda water

Smooth & Creamy

Method:

Place the brandy and milk in a shaker with two or three ice cubes and shake vigourously. Strain into a goblet or brandy snifter and add the soda water.

method:	SHAKER
glass:	GOBLET OR OVERSIZED WINE GLASS
garnish:	SPRINKLE OF NUTMEG

Egg Nogg

In the 17th century, Nog was a strong beer brewed in East Anglia in England; a noggin was a small mug of beer or liquor. In both England and the USA, a beaten egg was often added, and this seems to be the origin of Egg Nogg. Traditionally the drink of the holiday season from Christmas Eve to New Year's night, Egg Nogg tastes good any time. Today, there are as many arguments raging over the 'perfect Egg Nogg' as the 'perfect Mint Julep': some say an Egg Nogg should be 'liquid', others 'solid', to be eaten with a spoon; some advocate the whole egg, some just the yolk. Different schools of thought have given rise to numerous recipes, so here are just a couple. If you've never tried Egg Nogg, you're in for a real treat.

Ingredients:

1 measure brandy
1 measure dark rum
1½ measures milk
1 measure whipping cream
½ measure sugar syrup
1 small egg, beaten

Method:

Shake all the ingredients well in a shaker with two or three ice cubes or cracked ice. Strain and pour into a goblet and sprinkle with nutmeg.

If you reduce the rum to ½ a measure and add 1 measure of Madeira, you'll have yourself a Baltimore Egg Nogg.

method:	SHAKER
glass:	HIGHBALL OR OLD-FASHIONED
garnish:	WEDGE OF LIME AND SPRIG OF MINT

Ramos Fizz

The Ramos Fizz was the creation of Henrico C. Ramos in around 1888, when he arrived in New Orleans and bought the Imperial Cabinet Saloon. Ramos created a light, truly mouthwatering cocktail , the recipe for which was a closely guarded secret until the saloon closed in 1920, because of Prohibition, and Henrico's brother Charles Henry Ramos, finally revealed the ingredients. In honour of Henrico Ramos, why not make the Ramos Fizz on December 5th – the date that the Volstead Act (which brought in Prohibition in the USA) was repealed.

Smooth & Creamy

Method:

Pour all of the ingredients except the soda water into a shaker with half a cup of crushed ice. Shake vigourously. Strain and pour into an ice-filled glass – a highball if you want to add the soda, or an old-fashioned if you'd like just a squirt or none at all. Finish with soda water if desired, and garnish with the lime wedge and mint sprig. Serve with a straw and a stirrer.

Ingredients:

2 measures gin
1 dash sugar syrup
3 drops triple sec/ Cointreau
1 measure lemon juice
¾ measure lime juice
1 egg white
1 measure full cream mi[lk] or whipping cream
1 teaspoon powdered/ caster sugar
3 measures soda water (optional)

method:	SHAKER
glass:	COCKTAIL OR CHAMPAGNE SAUCER
garnish:	GRATED CHOCOLATE OR NUTMEG

Brandy Alexander

Originally, the Alexander was a gin-based drink, but the use of brandy has made it into one of the most sophisticated after-dinner drinks in spite of it's very simple construction. There are also a whole range of Alexanders that have been developed like the Coffee Alexander and Alexander's Sister, a treat if you like a mint flavour.

Ingredients:

1⅓ measures brandy
1⅓ measures dark creme de cacao
1⅓ measures double cream

Variations:

Rum Alexander:

Replace the brandy with 1 measure white rum, and ⅓ measure dark rum.

Amaretto Alexander:

Replace the brandy with 1⅓ measures amaretto.

Alexander's Sister:

Two measures gin, ⅔ measure green creme de menthe, 1⅓ measures double cream.

Gin Alexander:

Two measures gin, 1 measure white creme de cacao, 1 measure double cream.

Coffee Alexander:

One measure brandy, 1 measure Tia Maria or kahlua, 1 measure double cream.

Method:

Put two or three ice cubes into the shaker and add the creme de cacao and the cream. Next add the brandy and shake well. Strain into a cocktail glass or champagne saucer and decorate with grated chocolate or nutmeg.

method:	SHAKER
glass:	COCKTAIL
garnish:	GRATED CHOCOLATE

Angel's Treat

This cocktail is definitely one for the chocoholics!

Ingredients:

1½ measures dark rum
1 measure amaretto
1½ measures whipping cream
½ teaspoon sifted cocoa powder

Method:

Place all the ingredients into a shaker with two or three ice cubes and shake well. Strain and pour into a cocktail glass and decorate with chocolate flakes.

method:	BLENDER
glass:	PINA COLADA OR HURRICANE GLASS
garnish:	PINEAPPLE SLICE

Las Vegas

Like the town, it's over the top – but completely addictive!

Ingredients:

- 1 ½ measures tequila (gold, preferably)
- 2 measures coconut cream
- 2 measures orange juice
- 2 measures pineapple juice
- 1 measure whipping cream

Method:

Place half a glass of crushed ice in the blender and add the ingredients. Blend briefly and pour into a piña colada or hurricane glass. Garnish with the slice of pineapple and serve with straws.

If you replace the tequila with vodka, you'll have a Vodka Las Vegas.

method:	SHAKER
glass:	COCKTAIL
garnish:	TWO SLICES OF BANANA SPEARED EITHER SIDE OF A CHERRY

Banana Bliss

A creamy banana confection that always satisfies.

Smooth & Creamy

Method:

Put all the ingredients except the grenadine into a shaker with two or three ice cubes and shake well. Strain and pour into cocktail glass. Carefully pour the grenadine inside the rim of the glass so it runs down the inside leaving a red smear as it sinks to the bottom. Garnish with two slices of banana speared either side of a maraschino cherry.

Ingredients:

1¼ measures creme de banane
1¼ measures white rum
¾ measure orange juice
1¼ measures double cream
2 teaspoons grenadine
2 drops bitters

Barbary Coast

The Barbary Coast was the Mediterranean coastline of north Africa from Morocco to Libya and the home of pirates. That they ever drank this confection is highly unlikely: the drink dates from the 1920s, and originally, it was made without the rum.

Ingredients:

½ measure gin
½ measure white rum
½ measure Scotch
½ measure white creme de cacao
½ measure double cream

Method:

Place all the ingredients in a shaker with two or three ice cubes and shake vigourously. Strain into old-fashioned glass three-quarters filled with broken ice.

method:	BUILD
glass:	HIGHBALL
garnish:	STRAWBERRY AND MINT SPRIG

Fluffy Duck

This drink gives you the opportunity to use the Dutch speciality, Advocaat. Essentially it is a 'custom-made' egg nogg with a velvet texture and somewhat bland taste. In the Netherlands it is drunk as an aperitif and as a digestif, but it does mix well – and you can add it to a mug of hot chocolate at bedtime too!

Smooth & Creamy

Method:

Pour the rum and Advocaat into a highball glass, add the lemonade and mix well. Pour the cream carefully over the back of a spoon so it floats on top. Decorate with the strawberry and mint sprig and serve with straws and a stirrer.

Ingredients:

1 measure white rum
1 measure Advocaat
⅓ measure fresh cream
lemonade

method:	BUILD
glass:	COLLINS OR HIGHBALL
garnish:	CHERRY ON A STICK

Snowball

For most people a Snowball is a 'girlie' drink. This is largely because most people are deceived by the taste and think the drink has a low alcohol content. In fact the average alcohol content is about two units. There's nothing girlie about that!

Method:

Into a collins or highball glass, add some ice cubes. Pour in the Advocaat, add the lime cordial and top up with lemonade. Garnish with a cherry on a stick and serve with straws and a stirrer.

Ingredients:

2 measures Advocaat

¼ measure Rose's Lime Cordial

5 measures lemonade

method:	BUILD
glass:	GOBLET OR OVERSIZED WINE GLASS
garnish:	SLICE OF LEMON AND A CHERRY (TRADITIONALLY A GREEN CHERRY)

Dizzy Blonde

A delicious aniseed flavour that's enough to make any head spin!

Ingredients:

1¾ measures Advocaat
¾ measure Pernod
1 measure orange juice
2 measures lemonade

Smooth & Creamy

Method:

Fill a goblet three-quarters full with broken ice and pour in the Advocaat, Pernod, orange juice and top with lemonade. Garnish with the lemon slice and green cherry – a red one is okay too. Serve with straws and a stirrer and forget everything!

method:	SHAKER
glass:	CHAMPAGNE SAUCER OR COCKTAIL

Black Dublinski

Ireland meets Russia over coffee and a sherry!

Ingredients:

1 measure Baileys (Irish cream liqueur)

1 measure kahlua

1 measure vodka

½ measure dry sherry

Method:

Place all the ingredients in a shaker with two or three ice cubes and shake well. Strain into a cocktail glass or champagne saucer.

method:	SHAKER
glass:	GOBLET OR OVERSIZED WINE GLASS
garnish:	FRUIT IN SEASON

Caribbean Sunset

A fruity flavour and marvellous colour.

Ingredients:

1 measure creme de banane
1 measure gin
1 measure blue Curaçao
1 measure whipping cream
¾ measure lemon juice
⅓ measure grenadine

Smooth & Creamy

Method:

Place all the ingredients except the grenadine into a shaker with two or three ice cubes and shake well. Strain into a goblet filled with broken ice. Add the grenadine, allowing it to sink to the bottom and garnish with seasonal fruit.

method:	SHAKER
glass:	COCKTAIL

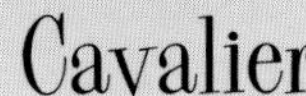

Cavalier

This has a delightful madarin-herb flavour.

Ingredients:

1 measure gold tequila
½ measure Galliano
2 measures mandarin juice
1 measure whipping cream

Method:

Place all the ingredients into a shaker with two or three ice cubes and shake well. Strain into a cocktail glass.

method:	SHAKER
glass:	FLUTE
garnish:	RASPBERRY OR A CHERRY ON A STICK

French Kiss

A subtle raspberry flavour.

Ingredients:

1 measure vodka

1 measure creme de framboise

½ measure Grand Marnier

1 measure whipping cream

Method:

Place all the ingredients into a shaker with two or three ice cubes and shake well. Strain and pour into a champagne flute and garnish with a fresh raspberry or a cherry on a stick.

Climax

One for the end of the evening perhaps?

Ingredients:

1½ measures Southern Comfort

1 measure kahlua

1 measure whipping cream

Method:

Place all the ingredients in a shaker with some broken ice and shake well. Pour, unstrained, into an old-fashion glass.

method:	SHAKER
glass:	COCKTAIL

Golden Dream

This cocktail was devised in 1960 by the makers of Galliano to promote the use of their golden yellow liqueur, the recipe for which is a very closely guarded secret.

Ingredients:

1 measure Galliano
1 measure triple sec/Cointreau
1 measure whipping cream
1 measure orange juice

Method:

Place all the ingredients in a shaker with two or three ice cubes and shake well. Strain into a cocktail glass and watch the sun rise.

method:	SHAKER
glass:	HIGHBALL
garnish:	CHERRY AND A SPRIG OF MINT

Lazy Days

This long, smooth, slow sipper is the perfect recipe for a relaxing summer evening.

Ingredients:

1 measure vodka
1 measure Tia Maria or Kahlua
1 measure Midori
⅓ measure green creme de menthe
1 ¼ measure whipping cream
2 measures lemonade

Method:

Place all the ingredients except the cream and the lemonade, in a shaker with two or three ice cubes and shake vigourously. Strain into ice-filled highball glass. Float whipped cream on top and garnish with the cherry and mint sprig.

method:	BLENDER
glass:	PINA COLADA, GOBLET OR HURRICANE

Love in the Afternoon

If you like strawberries, you'll love this – and you don't just have to reserve it for afternoons!

Smooth & Creamy

Method:

Keep a lovely strawberry aside for the garnish and place the other ingredients in the blender and blend until smooth. Add half a glass of crushed ice and blend briefly once more. Pour into a piña colada, goblet or hurricane glass and garnish with the strawberry. Serve with straws.

Ingredients:

2 measures dark rum
½ measure creme de fraise
1 measure orange juice
¾ measure coconut cream
½ measure sugar syrup
½ measure whipping cream
3 to 4 strawberries, plus one for garnish

method:	SHAKER
glass:	CHAMPAGNE SAUCER OR COCKTAIL
garnish:	CHERRY AND A SPRIG OF MINT

Grasshopper

*Sweet, minty, creamy – and delicately green! There's also a Flying Grasshopper too if you're into shooters (**see page 233**).*

Ingredients:

- 1⅓ measures white creme de menthe
- 1 measure green creme de menthe
- 1⅓ measures whipping cream

Smooth & Creamy

Method:

Place all the ingredients in a shaker with two or three ice cubes and shake well. Strain into a cocktail glass or champagne saucer and garnish with a sprig of mint. Serve with a short straw, if you wish.

Iced Delights

Frozen drinks are perfect summertime and party drinks and some – say with ice cream, a delicious liqueur and a topping of whipped cream – make for a very special dessert. These are the very adult equivalents of ice-cream sundaes!

There is a huge range of iced and 'frozen' drinks to enjoy: some are 'tropical' in nature and based on spirits and liqueurs blended with ice and served in tall glasses. Garnished with an accompanying assortment of seasonal fruits, theses drinks can be sipped slowly through a long straw while you lay back and dream of golden sands, blue skies and swaying palms trees on some distant coral island. Others are creamy confections, made with ice cream, and are guaranteed to cool you down just enough so you can turn up the heat!

All of the iced delights that follow are very simple to make in a food processor or blender but, for some, you will need a blender that is capable of handling ice. The secret of making iced drinks is to have everything – your equipment and your glasses as cold as possible and everything you need to 'build' the drinks – the spirits, liqueurs, mixers and the garnishes, ready prepared and set out for fast work. This will make sure that the drinks are as icy when you serve them as when you made them.

It is possible to make the drinks very quickly, then to pour into the chilled glasses and then 'set' in the ice box of your refrigerator for a few

Death by Chocolate

see page 205.

minutes before serving: but don't, whatever you do, put fine crystal glasses in the freezer or ice box as they might shatter. Add the garnishes – fruit, cream tops, straws, paper umbrellas – after you take the drinks out of the ice box and just before you serve them.

The beauty of these drinks is that you can vary the quantities to suit your own tastes: if, for example, you like your Frozen Daiquiri a little more 'sour', simply adjust the quantity of sugar or add a little more lime juice.

One of the easiest iced drinks to make – and enjoy – is the frappé. This is simply a 'short drink' poured over a glassful of crushed ice and served with short straws. You can use any single liqueur or spirit in a simple frappé – 2½ measures poured into a champagne saucer of crushed ice will be perfect. You will also find some further frappé recipes in the pages that follow to try for yourself.

Remember, however, that the recipes given do contain alcohol: 1 measure of rum, or brandy, or gin, or vodka or tequila is one unit of alcohol. With cocktails and mixed drinks, one glass equals, on average, two units of alcohol. So no matter how delicious they are, don't over do it!

Strawberry Dawn
see page 216.

method:	BUILD
glass:	LARGE COCKTAIL GLASS OR CHAMPAGNE SAUCER
garnish:	MARASCHINO CHERRY ON A STICK

Cafe Royale Frappe

This is a wonderfully elegant way to end dinner on a summer's evening.

Ingredients:

1 measure Cognac
3 measures cold black coffee
1 maraschino cherry

Iced Delights

Method:

Mix the coffee and the Cognac together in a mixing glass, and pour over a large cocktail glass full of crushed ice. Garnish with a cherry on a stick.

Try some of these other frappés:

London Fog

1¾ measures gin (that's the London part!) the fog is supplied by 1¾ measures anisette (substitute Pernod). Garnish with a slice of lemon.

Chocolate-orange Frappe

1½ measures dark creme de cacao, ¾ measure Grand Marnier, 1 measure orange juice.

Cognac-mint Frappe

1½ measures Cognac, ¾ measure white creme de menthe. Garnish with a mint sprig.

All-white Frappe

1 measure white creme de cacao, 1 measure Pernod, ½ measure white creme de menthe, ⅓ measure lime juice. Garnish with a cherry on a stick.

Fruit Frappe

1 measure white rum, ½ measure creme de banane, ¼ measure creme de cassis, 1 measure mandarin juice.

method:	BLENDER
glass:	BRANDY SNIFTER
garnish:	WHIPPED CREAM AND A CHERRY

Blue Cloud Cocktail

This really does look like a blue sky with fluffy white clouds! Think of the cherry as the 'red hot sun'!

Ingredients:

1 measure amaretto

½ measure blue Curaçao

2 measures vanilla ice cream

Method:

Combine all the ingredients in a blender and blend until smooth – the consistency of a thick milkshake. Pour into brandy snifter and top with whipped cream and the cherry.

method:	BLENDER
glass:	PARFAIT OR WHITE WINE GLASS
garnish:	FRESH STRAWBERRY

Blushin' Russian

The Russian is the vodka, the blush is the strawberry!

Ingredients:

1 measure coffee liqueur such as Tia Maria or kahlua
¾ measure vodka
1 scoop vanilla ice cream
5 large fresh strawberries (including one for the garnish)

Iced Delights

Method:

Put one strawberry aside for garnish. Combine all the ingredients in a blender and blend until smooth. Pour into a parfait or white wine glass and garnish with the strawberry – covered in chocolate if you wish!

method: BLENDER

glass: BRANDY SNIFTER

Canyon Quake

This is a delightfully creamy, brandy-almond flavour, and makes a wonderful dessert or after dinner drink.

Ingredients:

- ¾ measure Baileys (Irish cream liqueur)
- ¾ measure brandy
- 1 measure amaretto
- 2 measures fresh, single cream

Method:

Combine all the ingredients in a blender with two or three cracked ice cubes. Blend until smooth and pour into a large brandy snifter.

method:	BLENDER
glass:	RED WINE GLASS
garnish:	SLICE OF PINEAPPLE AND A CHERRY

Chi-chi

A very popular iced drink after a long day at the beach.

Ingredients:

1½ measures vodka

1 measure cream of coconut

4 measures pineapple juice

Method:

Blend all the ingredients with the glass of crushed ice at high speed in the blender. Pour into red wine glass and garnish with slice of pineapple and a cherry.

Cool Operator

method:	BLENDER
glass:	PARFAIT OR WHITE WINE GLASS
garnish:	MELON WEDGE AND A CHERRY

Ingredients:

1 measure Midori melon liqueur

½ measure lime juice

½ measure vodka

½ measure light rum

4 measures grapefruit juice

2 measures orange juice

Method:

Put all the ingredients in the blender and add ice to fill halfway. Blend until thick and pour into a parfait or white wine glass. Garnish with a wedge of melon and a cherry.

method: BLENDER

glass: PARFAIT OR WHITE WINE GLASS

Cranberry Cooler

Kentucky Derby Day isn't the only time to enjoy bourbon: try it in September as well, to celebrate National Bourbon Week!

Method:

Combine all the ingredients in a blender with a glass of crushed ice and blend until smooth. Pour into parfait or white wine glass and wait while your horse comes home.

Ingredients:

- 1½ measure bourbon
- 1½ measure cranberry juice
- ½ measure lime juice
- 1 teaspoon sugar

method:	BLENDER
glass:	PARFAIT OF WHITE WINE GLASS
garnish:	WHIPPED CREAM AND CHOCOLATE CURLS OR FLAKES

Death by Chocolate

What a way to go!

Ingredients:

1 measure Baileys (Irish cream liqueur)

½ measure dark creme de cacao

½ measure vodka

1 scoop chocolate ice cream

Method:

Combine the ingredients in the blender with a glass of crushed ice and blend until smooth. Pour into parfait or white wine glass. Garnish with whipped cream and sprinkle with grated chocolate curls or flakes of chocolate. Serve with a straw.

method:	BLENDER
glass:	FLUTE
garnish:	TWIST OF LIME PEEL

Devil's Tail

Just a little wicked!

Method:

Combine all the ingredients with half a glass of crushed ice in a blender and blend at low speed. Pour into the champagne flute and add the lime peel twist.

Ingredients:

1½ measure light rum
1 measure vodka
1 tablespoon lime juice
1½ tablespoon grenadine
1½ tablespoons apricot brandy

method:	BLENDER
glass:	PARFAIT OR WHITE WINE GLASS
garnish:	ORANGE SLICE

Di Amore Cream

This is perfect for Valentine's Day – or for sharing with a lover at any time!

Ingredients:

1½ measures amaretto
¾ measure white creme de cacao
2 measures orange juice
2 scoops vanilla ice cream

Method:

Combine all the ingredients in a blender and blend until smooth. Pour into parfait or white wine glass and garnish with a slice of orange.

method:	BLENDER
glass:	LARGE WINE GLASS
garnish:	MARASCHINO CHERRY

Frozen Steppes

Ingredients:

- 1 measure vodka
- 1 measure dark creme de cacao
- 1 scoop vanilla ice cream

Method:

Place all the ingredients in a blender and blend until smooth. Pour into a large wine glass and garnish with a maraschino cherry.

method:	BLENDER
glass:	FLUTE
garnish:	SPRIG OF MINT

Frozen Mint Daiquiri

Ingredients:

2 measures light rum

1 tablespoon lime juice

6 mint leaves,

1 teaspoon sugar

Method:

Combine all the ingredients in a blender with a glass of crushed ice and blend at low speed. Pour into the flute and decorate with a sprig of mint.

method:	SHAKER
glass:	LARGE CHAMPAGNE SAUCER
garnish:	LEMON SLICE

Frozen Blue Margarita

This is the frozen version of the famous tequila classic. Why not whizz a few up for Cinco de Mayo (5th May) to celebrate Mexico's national holiday.

Method:

Rim the glass with a little lemon juice and 'frost' the rim with salt. Place the ingredients in a shaker with two or three ice cubes. Shake and strain into a large champagne saucer filled with crushed ice and garnish with a slice of lemon.

Ingredients:

1¾ measures silver tequila
¾ measure blue Curaçao
¾ measure lemon juice
lemon juice
salt

method:	BLENDER
glass:	OLD-FASHIONED
garnish:	PINEAPPLE STICK

Frozen Matador

Ingredients:

1½ measures tequila
2 measures pineapple juice
1 tablespoon lime juice

Method:

Combine the ingredients in a blender with a glass of crushed ice and blend at low speed. Pour into an old-fashioned glass and garnish with a stick of pineapple.

method:	BLENDER
glass:	FLUTE
garnish:	STRAWBERRY

Gulf Stream

One for a special occasion... like a Wednesday!

Method:

Frost the rim of the flute with a little of the lime juice and dip into sugar. Combine the ingredients in a blender with some ice and blend until smooth. Pour into the sugar-rimmed champagne flute and garnish with a strawberry.

Ingredients:

1 measure blue Curaçao
3 measures champagne
½ measure light rum
½ measure brandy
1 measure lime juice
6 measures lemonade

method: BLENDER

glass: HIGHBALL

Hummer

A coffee-rum flavour that can be enjoyed at any time.

Ingredients:

1 measure Tia Maria or kahlua coffee liqueur
1 measure light rum
2 large scoops vanilla ice cream

Method:

Combine all the ingredients in a blender and blend briefly. Pour into a highball glass and serve with a straw.

method:	BLENDER
glass:	PARFAIT OR WHITE WINE GLASS

Italian Dream

Ingredients:

1½ measure Baileys (Irish cream liqueur)
½ measure Amaretto
2 measures fresh single cream

Method:

Combine all the ingredients in a blender with ice and blend until smooth. Serve in a parfait or white wine glass.

method:	BLENDER
glass:	PARFAIT OR WHITE WINE GLASS
garnish:	WHIPPED CREAM AND A CHERRY

Maraschino Cherry

Ingredients:

1 measure light rum
½ measure amaretto
½ measure peach schnapps
1 measure cranberry juice
1 measure pineapple juice
1 dash grenadine

Method:

Place all the ingredients in a blender with two to three glasses of ice and blend until smooth. Pour into parfait or white wine glass and top with whipped cream and a maraschino cherry.

method:	BLENDER
glass:	COCKTAIL
garnish:	STRAWBERRY AND SPRIG OF MINT

Strawberry Dawn

A lovely creamy cocktail with a delicate colour.

Method:

Keep one strawberry aside for garnish along with the mint sprig. Place all the ingredients into the blender with a glass of ice and blend at high speed. Pour into a cocktail glass and decorate with the strawberry and mint.

Ingredients:

1 measure gin
1 measure cream of coconut
5 fresh strawberries

method:	BLENDER
glass:	PARFAIT OR WHITE WINE GLASS
garnish:	SLICE OF ORANGE AND A CHERRY

Surf's Up

This frothy confection certainly looks like breaking waves.

Ingredients:

½ measure creme de banane
½ measure white creme de cacao
5 measures pineapple juice
1 measure single cream

Method:

Place the ingredients into a blender and blend until smooth. Pour into a parfait or white wine glass and garnish with the orange slice and the maraschino cherry.

method:	BLENDER
glass:	PILSNER
garnish:	PINEAPPLE WEDGE AND A CHERRY

The Big Chill

Chill out with one of these.

Ingredients:

1½ measures rum
1 measure pineapple juice
1 measure orange juice
1 measure cranberry juice
1 measure cream of coconut

Method:

Combine the ingredients with a glass of ice in a blender and blend until smooth. Pour into a pilsner glass and decorate with the pineapple wedge and the maraschino cherry.

method:	BLENDER
glass:	GOBLET
garnish:	SLICE OF LIME AND A CHERRY

Frozen Key Lime

A wonderfully sharp and tangy lime flavour.

Ingredients:

2 measures rum (light or dark, or try half and half)
1½ measures lime juice
3 tablespoons vanilla ice cream

Method:

Blend all the ingredients with half a glass of ice in a blender until smooth. Pour into a goblet and decorate with the lime slice and the cherry.

method:	BLENDER
glass:	FLUTE
garnish:	LIME WEDGE

Frozen Fuzzy

Try this Frozen Fuzzy on a hot day.

Iced Delights

Method:

Place the ingredients in a blender, fill with enough ice to reach the level of the liquid and blend. Pour into a champagne flute and garnish with a wedge of lemon.

Ingredients:

1 measure peach schnapps
½ measure triple sec/Cointreau
½ measure lime juice
½ measure grenadine
1 splash lemon-lime soda

method:	SHAKE WITH CRUSHED ICE
glass:	COCKTAIL OR CHAMPAGNE SAUCER

Scarlett O'Hara

Naturally, Southern Comfort is used for this pretty pink belle. The peachy flavour of Southern Comfort makes for terrific frozen sour-type drinks.

Ingredients:

2 measures Southern Comfort
1 measure grenadine
1 dash lime juice

Method:

Place a good scoop of crushed ice into a shaker and pour in the Southern Comfort, grenadine and the lime juice. Shake and pour, unstrained, into a cocktail or champagne saucer and serve with short straws.

method:	SHAKE WITH CRUSHED ICE
glass:	OLD-FASHIONED

Rhett Butler

You can't have Scarlet without Rhett – unless, of course, you frankly don't give a damn!

Ingredients:

2 measures Southern Comfort

¼ measure triple sec/Cointreau

¼ measure lime juice

¼ measure lemon juice

Method:

Put a good scoop of crushed ice into a shaker and add the Southern Comfort, triple sec/Cointreau, lemon and lime juices. Shake and pour, unstrained, into an old-fashioned glass and serve with a short straw.

method:	SHAKE WITH CRUSHED ICE
glass:	COCKTAIL
garnish:	MINT SPRIG (OPTIONAL)

Frozen Miami

Ingredients:

2½ measures light rum

½ measure white creme de menthe

½ measure lime juice

Variations:

Replace the creme de menthe with Cointreau and you'll have a Frozen Rum Side Car.

Method:

Place a good scoop of crushed ice in a shaker and add the rum, creme de menthe and lime juice. Shake briskly and pour, unstrained, into a cocktail glass. Garnish with a sprig of mint, serve with short straws and a shiver!

Shooters, Tooters and Pousse-cafes

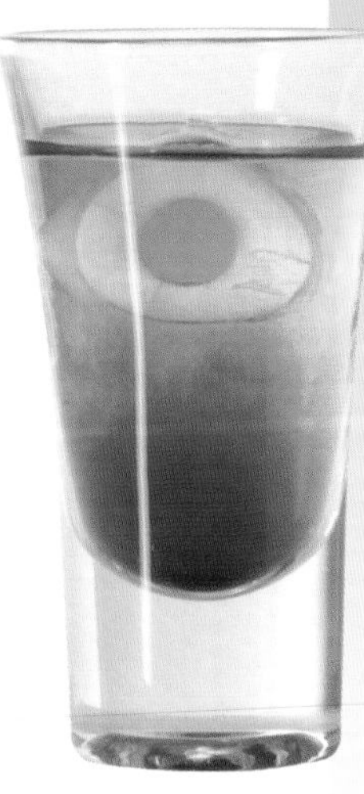

Ship's Cat
see page 250.

In the old Hollywood western movies, cowboys and outlaws swung by the saloon and downed a shot of whisky – or 'two fingers' (two ounces) in one swallow. Since then, shots – or shooters, tooters and slammers – are made with a huge range of wonderful spirits and mixers in bright, colourful concoctions with the most outrageous names and often decorated with a miniature garnish.

Shooters not only taste good, but they can be made up in large batches rather than in individual servings, so saving you time to enjoy them with friends at a party or celebration. Popular in many bars, bartenders have gone to great lengths to develop exciting new flavours and to develop themed drinks for special occasions and celebrations. You can serve shooters in shot glasses – of which there is a huge range of styles available, including the various 'novelty' shots in the shape of cowboy boots or wild animals. You can even get your own shot glass attached

Purple Hooter
see page 245.

to a necklace. Tooters are a new departure: in some bars they are served in a glass that looks remarkably like a laboratory test tube and are held in a rack, while in kitsch western-themed bars, staff carry tooters in holsters that look a little like the gun belts worn by cowboys in the movies. In place of bullets are the tooter tubes.

While many enjoy a wild night out with shooters and tooters, the drinks themselves are actually quite low in their alcohol content. Frequently the spirit or lower-proof liqueur is also combined with one or more juices, and the small size of the drinks themselves limits the amount of alcohol contained in each drink.

Some of the drinks on offer in this section are known as pousse–café or 'after–coffee'. A pousse–café is more a style of presentation, than a 'class' of drink as there are no common components, although drinks have been served in this style for centuries. Served after dinner, these cocktails consist of several liqueurs or spirits of specific gravities that sit in layers in the glass. The liqueurs must remain strictly separated, one above the other.

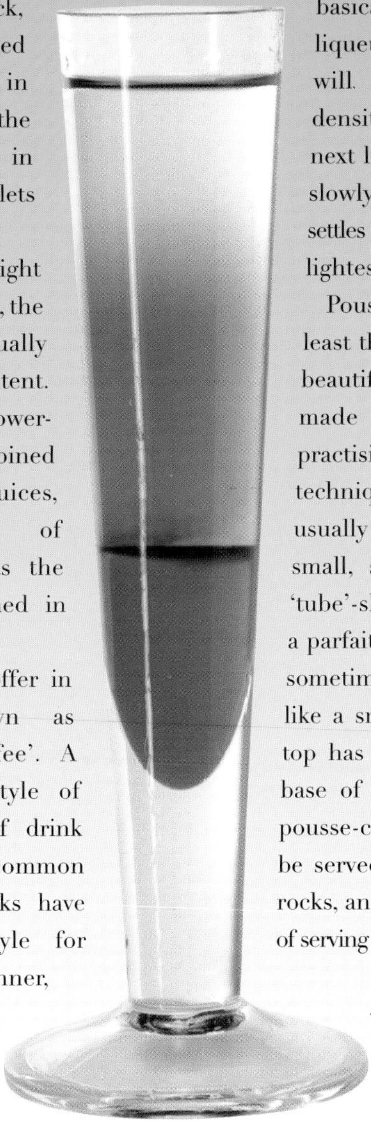

Each liquor has a different density: basically syrups are heavier than liqueurs, and spirits are lighter. You will need to pour the heaviest density into the glass first, then the next lightest is poured carefully and slowly over the back of a spoon so it settles in a separate layer, then the next lightest liquor is added.

Pousse-cafés traditionally have at least three layers, but there are some beautiful and delicious drinks to be made with just two : it's worth practising with these first to get your technique perfected. Pousse-cafés are usually served in their own glass: a small, straight-sided, short-stemmed 'tube'-shaped glass. You could also use a parfait glass or even a cordial glass – sometimes called a pony – which looks like a small white wine glass, but the top has a narrower opening than the base of the 'bowl'. Some well-known pousse-cafés – like the B–52 – may also be served stirred, strained and on the rocks, and you will find alternative ways of serving also suggested.

4th of July Tooter

see page 234.

method: MIXING GLASS

glass: SHOT

Alabama Slammer

Ingredients:

1 measure amaretto

1 measure Southern Comfort

½ measure sloe gin

1 splash lemon juice

Method:

Stir the amaretto, Southern Comfort and sloe gin with one or two ice cubes in a mixing glass. Strain into a shot glass and add the splash of lemon juice.

method:	BUILD
glass:	CORDIAL
garnish:	MARASCHINO CHERRY

Angel's Tip

This is a variation of the Prohibition era Angel's Tit, which was made with 1½ measures of maraschino and ⅔ measure fresh cream floated on top, garnished with a maraschino cherry to make a very suggestive cocktail. You can experiment with your favourite flavours.

Ingredients:

¾ measure creme de cacao (white)
¼ measure fresh cream

Method:

Pour the white creme de cacao into a cordial glass (no ice) and float the fresh cream carefully on top. Put the cherry on a cocktail stick and arrange so it sits naughtily on the top!

method: BUILD

glass: POUSSE-CAFE

B-52

This is one of those 'famous names' in cocktails and, while most people have heard of it, and most know that it was named after the huge B-52 transport planes developed for the US military, few will know that it is a coffee-flavoured drink with just a hint of orange to it.

Ingredients:

1 measure kahlua (coffee liqueur)

1 measure Baileys (Irish cream liqueur)

2 teaspoons Grand Marnier

Method:

Into a pousse–café glass, pour in the kahlua. Next, over the back of a spoon, carefully pour in the Baileys so it floats on top of the kahlua. Next, carefully add the Grand Marnier, so this sits on top of the Baileys. If it all goes wrong, don't despair: you can stir and strain all the ingredients into an ice-filled old-fashioned glass and it will taste equally delicious!

Blue Marlin

The smoothness of the rum combined with the sweet orange flavour of the Curaçao and balanced by the sharpness of the fresh lime juice is a delight. Curaçao comes in a range of 'novelty' colours in addition to the clear, colourless version, but the flavour is always orange. The bright blue Curaçao used here goes someway in explaining an old Arabic saying in Tunisia, North Africa, which goes 'The land is blue like an orange'!

Ingredients:

1 measure light rum
½ measure blue Curaçao
1 measure lime juice

Method:

Stir the light rum, blue Curaçao and lime juice in a mixing glass with two or three ice cubes. Strain into a shot glass.

method:	BUILD
glass:	SHOT
garnish:	SMALL LIME WEDGE

Bloody Caesar Shooter

Not only delicious, but there's the added bonus of a surprise tasty treat at the bottom of the glass. If you feel like pushing the boat out, put an oyster in instead of the clam – but you may need to use a larger glass!

Ingredients:

1 clam (or oyster)

1 measure vodka

1½ measures tomato juice

2 drops Worcestershire sauce

2 drops Tabasco sauce

1 dash horseradish

Celery salt

Method:

Put the clam (or oyster) in the bottom of the glass. Add the Worcestershire sauce, Tabasco and horseradish. Add the vodka and tomato juice, sprinkle with celery salt and garnish with a small wedge of lime.

C.C. Kazi

Ingredients:

1½ measures tequila

2 measures cranberry juice

1 teaspoon lime juice

Method:

Into a shaker with some ice cubes, add the lime juice, cranberry juice and tequila. Shake and strain into a cordial glass.

method: SHAKER
glass: CORDIAL

Capri

This is the adult equivalent of a banana split: the white chocolate flavour of the creme de cacao combined with creme de banane and topped by fresh cream. Instead of a dessert, try one of these instead!

Method:

Place the ingredients into a shaker with a few ice cubes. Shake well and strain into a cordial glass.

Ingredients:

¾ measure white creme de cacao
¾ measure creme de banane
¾ measure fresh cream

Flying Grasshopper

Related to the creamy-minty cocktail called the Grasshopper this 'high-flying' version is kick started by vodka

Ingredients:

¾ measure green creme de menthe

¾ measure white creme de cacao

¾ measure vodka

Method:

In a mixing glass with ice, stir together the creme de menthe, creme de cacao and the vodka. Strain into a cordial glass.

method:	BUILD
glass:	POUSSE-CAFE, SHOT OR CORDIAL GLASS

4th of July Tooter

You can have this on Independence Day, 4th July, and then 10 days later on Bastille Day to celebrate the French national day. Numerous countries have national flag colours of red, white and blue, so you could raise a glass to them as well!

Ingredients:

1 measure grenadine
1 measure blue Curaçao
1 measure vodka

Method:

Into a shot, pousse-café or cordial glass, carefully add the ingredients in the order stated above, so that they float one on top of the other.

Variations:

How about an Italia: First level: mix ¾ measure of grenadine and 1 teaspoon of cherry brandy. Second level: mix ¾ measure of anisette and 1 teaspoon white creme de menthe. Third level: 1 measure yellow Chartreuse with a few dashes of blue Curaçao, to make the green part of the flag. Mix the three 'colours' first then pour each carefully into the glass: red first, then white, then green. *Salute!*

method:	SHAKER
glass:	CORDIAL OR COCKTAIL

Foxy Lady

Dark and seductive with a chocolate-almond flavour.

Ingredients:

1 measure amaretto

½ measure dark (brown) creme de cacao

1 measure thick fresh cream

Method:

Place all the ingredients in a shaker with two or three ice cubes. Shake well and strain into a cordial glass, or cocktail glass if you prefer.

method:	SHAKER
glass:	SHOT

Galactic Ale

This fruity recipe will serve two: one for you and one for you, in a parallel universe.

Ingredients:

1¼ measures vodka

1¼ measure blue Curaçao

1 measure lime juice

½ measure creme de framboise (raspberry liqueur)

Method:

In a shaker with two to three ice cubes, shake all the ingredients vigourously. Then strain into two shot glasses. Live long and prosper.

Green Demon

A chance to use one of the most idiosyncratic liqueurs, the melon-flavoured Midori, which, in Japanese, means 'green'.

Ingredients:

½ measure vodka
½ measure light rum
½ measure Midori (melon liqueur)
½ measure lemonade

Method:

In a shaker with two or three ice cubes, shake the vodka, rum and Midori. Add the lemonade to the shaker – do not shake but stir twice. Strain into shot glass.

method: SHAKER

glass: SHOT

Hay Fever Remedy

I find I feel better instantly!

Ingredients:

½ measure vodka

¼ measure Southern Comfort

¼ measure amaretto

½ measure pineapple juice

1 teaspoon grenadine

Method:

Shake all the ingredients with two or three ice cubes in a shaker. Strain into a shot glass.

Honolulu Shooter

The delightfully fruity shooter could be made into a longer drink and served on the rocks if you prefer – simply adjust the quantities of the juices to suit your taste and create your own paradise island.

Ingredients:

1 measure gin
1 teaspoon pineapple juice
1 teaspoon orange juice
1 teaspoon lemon juice
1 teaspoon of pineapple syrup
1 drop angostura bitters

Method:

Shake all the ingredients vigourously in a shaker with two or three ice cubes. Strain into a shot glass.

Irish Charlie

Try this on St. Patrick's Day.

Ingredients:

1 measure Baileys (Irish cream liqueur)
1 measure white creme de menthe

Method:

Put two or three ice cubes in a mixing glass.
Add the Baileys and creme de menthe and stir.
Strain into a cordial glass.

Johnny on the Beach

This recipe will serve two beach bums and keep them happy until surf's up.

Ingredients:

1½ measures vodka
1 measure Midori (melon liqueur)
1 measure creme de framboise (raspberry liqueur)
½ measure pineapple juice
½ measure orange juice
½ measure grapefruit juice
½ measure cranberry juice

Method:

In a mixing glass with two or three ice cubes, add the ingredients and stir. Strain into two shot glasses.

method:	SHAKER
glass:	CORDIAL
garnish:	MELON BALL (OPTIONAL)

Melon Ball

If you like Midori, you'll love this.

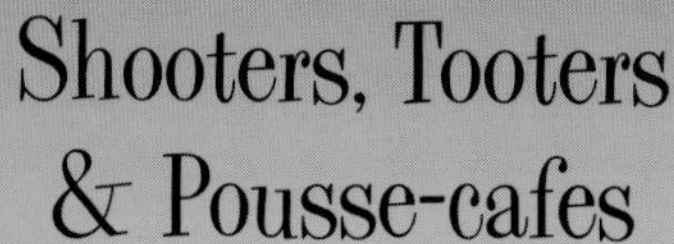

Method:

Shake all the ingredients with ice then strain into a cordial glass. Garnish, if you wish, with a melon ball.

Ingredients:

1 measure Midori (melon liqueur)
1 measure vodka
1 measure pineapple juice

Oh My Gosh

This is a wonderful wintertime warmer – especially if you've just come in from the cold.

Ingredients:

I measure peach schnapps
I measure amaretto

Method:

Add two to three ice cubes to a mixing glass. Pour in the peach schnapps and amaretto and stir. Strain into shot glass.

method: SHAKER
glass: CORDIAL

Peppermint Pattie

Very simple to make but a wonderful subtle chocolate-mint flavour.

Ingredients:

I measure white creme de menthe

I measure white creme de cacao

Method:

Place the ingredients in a shaker with some ice cubes. Shake and strain into cordial glass.

Purple Hooter

Gorgeous colour and great taste too.

Ingredients:

1½ measures vodka (try a citrus vodka if you want!)
½ measure triple sec or Cointreau
¼ measure creme de framboise (raspberry liqueur)

Method:

Shake the ingredients with two to three ice cubes in a shaker and strain into a chilled shot glass.

method:	BUILD
glass:	POUSSE-CAFE OR CORDIAL GLASS

Rattlesnake

Another pousse-café for you to try with your steady hand! This has a lovely whisky-chocolately-coffee flavour, perfect for after dinner.

Ingredients:

I measure kahlua

I measure Baileys (Irish cream liqueur)

I measure white creme de cacao

Method:

In a pousse-café or cordial glass, add the kahlua. Next pour the Baileys slowly over the back of a spoon so it floats on top of the kahlua. Finally, carefully pour the white creme de cacao over the back of a spoon so it floats on the Baileys.

Rocky Mountain

Try this subtle combination of peachy-whiskey with almonds.

Ingredients:

1 measure Southern Comfort

1 measure amaretto

½ measure lime juice

Method:

Shake all the ingredients in a shaker with two or three ice cubes. Strain into a shot glass.

method:	SHAKER WITH CRACKED ICE, OR IN A BLENDER
glass:	CORDIAL

Scooter

You can make this in a blender or shaker: it's a perfect post-dinner drink that you could have in lieu of a dessert!

Ingredients:

I measure brandy

I measure amaretto

I measure fresh cream

Method:

Combine all the ingredients in a blender, or shake with some cracked ice and strain into a cordial glass.

Sex on the Beach

One of those drinks that everyone knows the name of, but few dare to ask for! Now's your chance to try it in the privacy of your own home with 20 or 30 or your very closest friends!

Ingredients:

½ measure creme de framboise (raspberry liqueur)
½ measure Midori (melon liqueur)
½ measure vodka
1 measure pineapple juice
cranberry juice

Method:

In a mixing glass with two or three ice cubes, stir all the ingredients except the cranberry juice. Strain into cordial glass and top with the cranberry juice.

method: BUILD

glass: SHOT

Ship's Cat

In the UK, this shooter is often made with Vimto – an odd, though popular, purple-coloured fruit cordial that is diluted with water. If you don't have a bottle of Vimto handy, substitute with creme de cassis. In both cases you'll have a delightfully fruity-rum flavoured drink.

Ingredients:

1 measure over-proof dark rum

1 teaspoon Vimto or creme de cassis

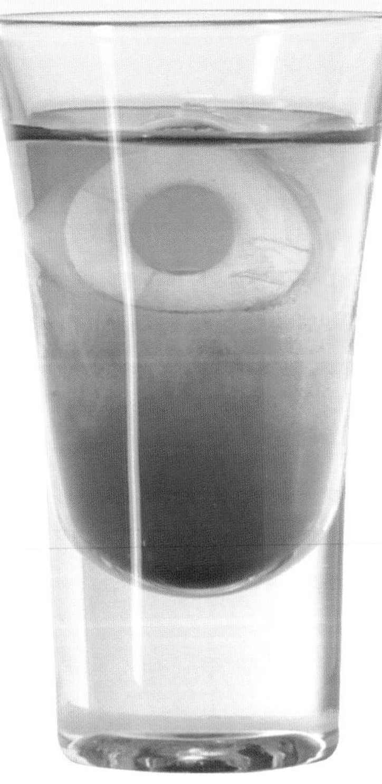

Method:

Put one ice cube in a shot glass, add the Vimto or creme de cassis and the rum.

Silver Spider

Ingredients:

½ measure light rum
½ measure vodka
½ measure triple sec or Cointreau
½ measure white creme de menthe

Method:

Place all the ingredients in a mixing glass with two or three ice cubes and stir. Strain into a shot glass.

method: SHAKER

glass: SHOT

Teeny Weeny Woo Woo

Ingredients:

½ measure vodka

½ measure peach schnapps

1 measure cranberry juice

Method:

Shake with two or three ice cubes in a shaker then strain into a shot glass.

Index

Bibliography

Calabrese, Salvatore. *Classic Cocktails*, Prion, 1997.

Costantino, Maria. *The Cocktail Handbook*, D&S Books, 2001.

Cross, Robert. *The Classic 1,000 Cocktails,* Foulsham, 1996.

Embury, David A. *The Fine Art of Mixing Drinks*, Faber, 1963.

Faith, Nicholas, and Ian Wisniewski. *Classic Vodka*, Prion, 1996.

Heath, Ambrose. *Good Drinks*, Faber 1939.

Jackson, Michael. *Michael Jackson's Pocket Bar Book*, Mitchell Beazley, 1981.

MacElhone, Harry. *Harry's ABC of Mixing Cocktails*, Souvenir Press, 1986.

Marcialis, Gino, and Franco Zingales. *The Cocktail Book,* MacDonald, 1983.

Murray, Jim. *Classic Bourbon, Tennessee and Rye Whiskey*, Prion, 1997.

Regan, Gary. *The Bartender's Bible,* HarperCollins, 1993.

Acknowledgements

Thanks to Robert de Niet for glasses – and for some of his favourite recipes.